PRONOUNCE IT
PERFECTLY
IN ENGLISH

by Jean Yates

Northern Virginia
Community College

 انتشارات زبانکده
نماینده انحصاری انتشارات LONGMAN درایران
مرکز فروش وپخش انواع کتب و نوارهای Higher Education, E.L.T
و جدیدترین متد سمعیو بصریآموزش زبان
تهران ـ میدان انقلاب ـ بازارچه کتاب ـ شماره۸ تلفن: ۶۴۰۲۳۶۷ فکس: ۶۴۹۲۹۶۱
e-mail zabankadeh @ sinasoft.net
صندوق پستی ۵۶۴ ـ ۱۳۱۴۵

BARRON'S

BARRON'S EDUCATIONAL SERIES, INC.

All inquiries should be addressed to:
Barron's Educational Series, Inc.
250 Wireless Boulevard
Hauppauge, NY 11788

International Standard Book No. 0-8120-9118-3

Library of Congress Catalog Card No. 95-12841

Library of Congress Cataloging-in-Publication Data

Yates, Jean.
    Pronounce it perfectly in English / by Jean Yates.
        p. cm. — (Pronounce it perfectly in—)
    ISBN 0-8120-8244-3 (bk./cassettes pkg.).— ISBN
0-8120-9118-3 (book only). — ISBN 0-8120-9119-1
(cassette #1). — ISBN 0-8120-9120-5 (cassette #2).
— ISBN 0-8120-9585-5 (cassette #3)
    1. English language—Pronunciation for foreign
speakers—Problems, exercises, etc. I. Title.
II. Series.
PE1137.Y38 1995
428.3'4—dc20   95-12841
                                                CIP

PRINTED IN THE UNITED STATES OF AMERICA
5678 9770 98765

CONTENTS

کد ۱۸۱

انتشارات فروزش

تیراژ: ۳۰۰۰ جلد   نوبت چاپ: سوم ۱۳۸۲

لیتوگرافی: تصویر   قیمت: ۹۰۰۰ ریال

ناشر: انتشارات فروزش

دفتر و فروشگاه مرکزی- تبریز - خیابان امام خمینی - سه راه طالقانی
ساختمان جام جم - طبقه اول و دوم - صندوق پستی   ۲۵۸۵ - ۵۱۳۲۵
تلفاکس: ۵۵۵۳۰۷۹۲ - ۵۵۵۶۷۳۲ - ۵۵۶۶۳۲۲ (۰۴۱۱)
فروشگاه شماره (۱): تبریز - چهار راه آبرسان، روبروی هلال احمر
تلفن: ۲۲۶۱۳۱۷ - ۲۲۶۲۹۲۹ (۰۴۱۱)
دفتر پخش: تهران - خیابان وحید نظری - پلاک ۲۵۰
تلفن: ۶۴۹۳۱۳۸ (۰۲۱) فاکس: ۶۴۶۱۴۶۰ (۰۲۱)

Introduction

The goal of "perfect pronunciation" is not to take your personality out of your speech. Indeed, mannerisms that give hints of your origin are charming in English. The goal is, rather, to speak so that people listen to *what* you say, not *how* you say it. The goal is to be understood the first time you say something, and to be confident and proud of the way you speak.

This book and tape are designed to help you pronounce English words, phrases, and sentences correctly, so that the meaning you intend is clear and the sounds are pleasing to the ear.

The materials are organized to help you get through the maze of English spelling so that you will know how to pronounce any new word. English spelling reflects the history of the words rather than how they are pronounced. The spelling of the vowel sounds, in particular, is an unreliable guide to their pronunciation. Also, many vowel and consonant letters are silent; they are simply not pronounced at all. Most importantly, however, the pronunciation of many grammatical markers systematically changes according to the sounds that precede them, and these changes are not reflected in the spelling. Native speakers do not even notice these changes, but make them automatically. You will learn to do the same thing.

The book is divided into four parts: Vowel Sounds, Consonant Sounds, Stress Patterns, and Intonation Patterns. Each sound is considered separately, by sound rather than by spelling. There are instructions and diagrams to show you how the sound is made. Examples are given of the sound in all possible positions in a word or phrase, and examples are given of all possible spellings of the sound. The unique stress and intonation patterns of English, which often carry meaning, are described in detail, with examples for practice. The tapes include all of these examples, modeled by native speakers, with pauses provided so that you can repeat them. The book and tape also include exercises, quizzes, and practice material to help you make sure you are hearing and producing the sounds correctly.

As the pronunciation of grammatical markers is vital for understanding, there are sections entitled "Usage Tips" throughout the materials. Pay particular attention to these sections. If you are a beginner or have trouble making yourself understood, do these sections first, and continue to practice them.

Do not be discouraged if at first you do not hear the differences in sounds. You can train yourself to hear them. Follow the instructions for making the sounds; check yourself by looking in the mirror; tape-record your voice. Practice making the differences and you will begin to hear them.

The book and audio cassettes are coordinated so that you can use them separately or together. To improve your understanding of English spelling and your recognition of written words, listen to the tape while looking at the words and sentences in the book. When you listen to the tape without the book, simply repeat the examples during the pauses provided for writing, and do the written exercises later.

The symbols used to represent each sound are based on those of the International Phonetic Alphabet. Because many English vowel sounds are combinations of sounds, they are represented here by combinations of symbols. This is intended to help the learner form these sounds by combining their individual parts.

The pronunciation symbols used by *The American Heritage Dictionary*, *The Random House Dictionary*, *The Merriam-Webster Dictionary*, *The Oxford Dictionary*, and *Longman's Dictionary* appear below, so that you may use this book as a pronunciation guide for any new word you look up in your own dictionary.

Guide to Symbols

Unit	Barron's	Longman's	Oxford	Random House	American Heritage	Merriam Webster
1	ə	ə	e o i a u	ə	ə	ə
2	ɪ	ɪ	ĭ	i	ĭ	i
3	u	ʊ	ŏŏ	ŏŏ	ŏŏ	u̇
4	iy	iʸ	ē	e	ē	ē
5	uw	uʷ	ōō	ōō	ōō	ü
6	iuw	ju	ū	yōō	iu	yü
7	ʌ	ʌ	ŭ	u	ŭ	'ə
8	ɛ	e	ĕ	e	ĕ	e
9	ow	əʊ	ō	ō	ō	ō
10	oiy	ɔɪ	oi	oi	oi	ȯi
11	eə	eə	ĕ	â	â	a
12	eiy	eɪ	ā	ā	ā	ā
13	ɔ	ɔ	aw	ô	ô	ȯ
14	æ	æ	ă	a	ă	a
15	æow	aʊ	ow	ou	ou	au̇
16	a	a	ah	ä	ŏ	ä
17	aiy	aɪ	ī	ī	ī	ī
18	p b	p b	p b	p b	p b	p b
19	t d	t d	t d	t d	t d	t d
20	k g	k g	k g	k g	k g	k g
21	f v	f v	f v	f v	f v	f v
22	ch j	tʃ dʒ	ch j	ch j	ch j	ch j
23	sh zh	ʃ ʒ	sh zh	sh zh	sh zh	sh zh
24	s z	s z	s z	s z	s z	s z
25	l r	l r	l r	l r	l r	l r
26	m n ŋ	m n ŋ	m n ng	m n ng	m n ng	m n ŋ
27	θ ð	θ ð	th dh	th t͟h	th t͟h	th t͟h
28	h	h	h	h	h	h
29	w y	w j	w y	w y	w y	w y

Acknowledgement: The quotation from MY FAIR LADY on page 38, by permission of the Estate of Alan Jay Lerner © 1956 by Alan Jay Lerner and Frederick Loewe.

PART ONE
English Vowel Sounds

Every vowel sound represents a syllable in a word.

Syllables are either emphasized and "stressed," or weak and "unstressed."

There are 17 different vowel sounds in English.

They all have "voice," which occurs as the vocal cords vibrate.

The tongue does not touch other parts of the mouth, teeth, or lips.

The vowel sounds differ by

- the distance between the lips
- the shape of the lips
- the length of time the sound is held

The vowel sounds are ordered in this book according to how open the mouth is. The first sound, /ə/, is made with the mouth almost closed. As the lessons progress, the mouth gradually opens. The final sound, /aiy/, is made with the mouth wide open.

To pronounce each vowel correctly, follow these steps:

- Look in the mirror.
- Compare your mouth with each diagram.
- Make short sounds quickly.
- Count to two, silently, for long sounds.

Introducing the Sound

The /ə/ is one of the most common sounds in English.

To make it, open your mouth very slightly; your lips should be about ⅛ inch (3 mm) apart; relax your lips; make a short sound with your voice. (See Figure 1.)

/ə/ in Unstressed Syllables

Figure 1.
The sound /ə/.

Almost every unstressed syllable in English is pronounced /ə/. This sound can be spelled with any of the vowel letters, <u>a</u>, <u>e</u>, <u>i</u>, <u>o</u>, <u>u</u>, or any combination of these letters. Hereafter, in the Examples and Exercise Sections, the letters of unstressed syllables that should be pronounced /ə/ will be printed in *italics*. This will identify them while preserving their correct spelling.

Listen to the following examples of words with the sound /ə/ in unstressed syllables and repeat them after the speaker.

EXAMPLES

a-go	so-d*a*	cap-t*ai*n
*e*f-fect	o-p*e*n	pi-g*eo*n
*e*x-plain	den-*i*m	par-t*ia*l
*o*c-cur	meth-*o*d	sta-t*io*n
u-pòn	syr-*u*p	cup-b*oa*rd

Usage Tip

• The words <u>a</u>, <u>an</u>, and <u>the</u> are articles, unstressed words that occur before nouns and adjective-noun combinations. Say them quickly, without emphasis. Pronounce the vowel as /ə/.

Listen to the following examples of articles containing the /ə/ sound, and repeat them after the speaker.

EXAMPLES

a book	*a*n appl*e*	th*e* book
a cat	*a*n or*a*nge	th*e* cat
a dog	*a*n ice cube	th*e* dog
		th*e* un*i*verse

(When <u>the</u> occurs before a word beginning with a vowel sound, the <u>e</u> is pronounced /iy/. (See Unit Four, page 10.)

/ə/ in Stressed Syllables

When /ə/ is followed by the consonant /r/, it can be the prominent, or *stressed* vowel of a word. In the examples that follow, and throughout the rest of this book, the sound that is being introduced will be printed in **boldface** type.

Listen to the examples and repeat them after the speaker.

EXAMPLES

urn	earn	work
fur	heard	worm
purse	yearns	
		tourn-*a*-ment
serve	bird	
nerve	girl	syr-*u*p
	first	

Practice for Mastery

Listen to the following sentences that feature the sound /ə/, and repeat them after the speaker.

EXAMPLES

> I heard her journey was worth the worry.
> The sugar was the color of earth.
> The early bird gets the worm.

Continue to practice this sound while learning the rest of the vowel sounds. Remember that the /ə/ sound will be written in *italics* when it occurs in unstressed syllables.

Introducing the Sound

To make the /ɪ/ sound, lower your jaw slightly. The lips are relaxed and are about ¼ inch (6 mm) apart. (See Figure 2.)

The sound is short.

Figure 2.
The sound /ɪ/.

Listen to the examples and repeat them after the speaker.

EXAMPLES

if	gym	pretty	busy
in	symbol	English	
big			women
miss		sieve	
build			

Practice for Mastery

Listen to the following sentences featuring the vowel sound /ɪ/ and repeat them after the speaker.

Examples

> Jim is in the picture.
> Miss Smith is thin.
> Bring chicken for dinner.
> Listen to this ridiculous list.
> The pretty women are busy in the gym.

Introducing the Sound

This vowel is formed by keeping the jaw slightly open. The lips are ¼ inch (6 mm) apart and pushed outward to make an open circle. (See Figure 3.)

The sound is short.

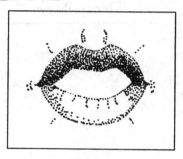

Figure 3.
The sound /u/.

Listen to the examples and repeat them after the speaker.

EXAMPLES

| put | look | could | wom*a*n |
| push | book | would | wolf |

Practice for Mastery

Listen to the following sentences featuring the sound /u/, and repeat them after the speaker.

8

EXAMPLES

Look in the cookbook for *a* good pudding.
He would if he could.
It should be good wool.
The woman took *a* good look *at* the wolf.

Introducing the Sound

To make this sound, set your lips ⅜ inch (1 cm) apart. Widen your lips into a big smile. (See Figure 4.)

The sound is long. Count to two silently to be sure it is long enough.

Figure 4.
The sound /iy/.

Listen to the following examples and repeat them after the speaker.

EXAMPLES

be	key	people	ski
he	honey		police
we		*a*moeb*a*	
	cheap	آ ی با	suite
bee	fear	ei**th**er	
see		receive	chassis چ سی
sweet			d*e*bris
			دبری
		niece	
		نی س	chamois
			شمٌی

Usage Tips

- The <u>e</u> in the article <u>the</u> is pronounced /iy/ when it is followed by a word beginning with a vowel sound.

Listen to the examples and repeat them after the speaker.

EXAMPLES

the apple	the orange	the ocean
the elephant	the onion	the umpire
the ice		

- The /iy/ sound, spelled <u>y</u> at the end of a word often indicates an adjective.

Listen to the examples and repeat them after the speaker.

EXAMPLES

tricky	soapy	sticky	heavy
edgy	chilly	shaky	easy

- Adverbs often end in the syllable <u>ly</u>, pronounced /liy/.

Listen to the examples and repeat them after the speaker.

EXAMPLES

nicely	quickly	slowly
plainly	sweetly	clearly

- A final /iy/ sound after a name can indicate endearment or informality.

Listen to the examples and repeat them after the speaker.

EXAMPLES

sweetie	Susie	daddy
Bŏbby	mŏmmy	cutie

Practice for Mastery

Listen to the following sentences featuring the vowel sound /iy/ and repeat them after the speaker.

EXAMPLES

Jeannie, do you see the bees?
Please freeze the peas.
Neither he nor she believes me.
We can easily read the agreement.

Contrasting Sound Practice

Compare the sound /ɪ/ from Unit Two with the sound /iy/, by repeating the following words after the speaker.

EXAMPLES

/ɪ/	/iy/	/ɪ/	/iy/
bit	beet	rich	reach
sit	seat	pick	peak, peek
rip	reap	dim	deem
lip	leap	dip	deep
live	leave	sin	seen, scene
did	deed	fist	feast
hill	heel, heal, he'll	sis	cease
mill	meal	his	he's
pill	peel, peal	ship	sheep
lick	leak, leek	chip	cheap

Now listen to several sentences that feature both sounds, and repeat them after the speaker.

EXAMPLES

> Six sheep were sick on the ship.
> Jim eats cheap chips.
> He leaves me this measly little meal.
> She's as thin as he is.
> Please peel the beets and string the beans.

Recognition Practice

The speaker will pronounce five words featuring these sounds. During the pauses, circle the word you hear. If it is not convenient for you to write at this time, use the pauses to repeat the words after the speaker, then complete the written exercise later. The correct answers appear below.

EXERCISE

1. sin   scene
2. live   leave
3. his   he's
4. hill   he'll
5. sit   seat

Dictation Practice

Now the speaker will pronounce five words featuring these two sounds. During the pauses, write each word on a piece of paper. If it is not convenient for you to write at this time, use the pauses to repeat the words after the speaker, then complete the written exercise later. The correct answers appear below.

Answers to Exercises

Recognition Practice, scene, live, his, he'll, seat
Dictation Practice, dip, meal, reach, sin, he's

او

Introducing the Sound

To make the /uw/ sound, keep the mouth slightly open and the lips ⅜ inch (1 cm) apart. The lips are tense, and pushed forward into a small circle. (See Figure 5.)

The sound is long.

Figure 5.
The sound /uw/.

Listen to the examples and repeat them after the speaker.

EXAMPLES

do	loose	flu	due	flew
lose	choose	rude	blue	new
who	food		Tuesday	نمو
two				
canoe	through	juice	rheumatism	lieu
shoe	soup			

14

Practice for Mastery

Listen to the following sentences featuring the sound /uw/ and repeat them after the speaker.

EXAMPLES

> Sue knew the truth.
> Choose blue for the new room.
> It blooms soon, in June.
> The news is too gloomy.

Contrasting Sound Practice

Now compare the sound /u/ from Unit Three with the sound /uw/. Listen and repeat each word after the speaker.

EXAMPLES

/u/	/uw/	/u/	/uw/
full	fool	pull	pool
stood	stewed	cookie	kooky
would, wood	wooed	nook	nuke
hood	who'd		

Now repeat the following sentences, which feature both vowel sounds.

EXAMPLES

> Lou couldn't fool Sue.
> Stu wouldn't move the cooking school.
> The good pool room is booked for Tuesday
>   at noon.
> The cook stood and looked at his new shoes.

Recognition Practice

The speaker will pronounce five words. In your book, circle the ones you hear, or repeat them now and do the written exercise later. The correct answers appear below.

EXERCISE

1. hood   who'd
2. full   fool
3. wood   wooed
4. nook   nuke
5. stood   stewed

Dictation Practice

Write the next five words recorded on the tape on a piece of paper, or repeat them during the pauses and write the exercise later. The correct answers appear below.

Keep in mind that learning to make the sounds correctly and practicing them will help you to hear their differences.

Spelling Challenge

Four sentences containing words with tricky spelling are next recorded on the tape. Write them down during the pauses, then check your work below. If it is not convenient for you to write at this time, repeat the sentences during the pauses, and write them later.

Answers to Exercises

Recognition Practice, hood, full, wooed, nook, stewed
Dictation Practice, who'd, stood, pool, would, full
Spelling Challenge, I see a big woman and two little women.
We drank sweet juice in the hotel suite. It's good food.
Don't shoot him in the foot.

Introducing the Sound

The /iuw/ sound is a combination of the sounds /iy/ and /uw/. The lips are ⅜ inch (1 cm) apart. Begin with the lips spread into a big smile, then push them forward into a circle. (See Figure 6.)

The sound is short.

Figure 6.
The sound /iuw/.

Listen to the examples and repeat them after the speaker.

EXAMPLES

use	yew	view	beauty
cute	few		
music		feud	you
	ewe		
			hue

When /iuw/ occurs in unstressed syllables, the second sound of the combination changes from /uw/ to /ə/. Begin with the lips ⅜ inch apart, and make the /iy/ sound. Move the lips to the almost-closed and relaxed position of /ə/.

Listen to the examples and repeat them after the speaker.

EXAMPLES

figure	union	medium	accurate
failure	usually		accusation
			immunize
	canyon		
			your

Usage Tip

• Use the article <u>a</u> (pronounced /ə/) instead of <u>an</u> before words beginning with this sound.

Listen to the examples and repeat them after the speaker.

EXAMPLES

This is *a* universal truth.
It is *a* university in New York.
They will form *a* union.
This is *a* usual occurrence.

Practice for Mastery

Listen to the following sentences featuring the sound /iuw/, and repeat them after the speaker.

EXAMPLES

A few beauties were in the picture.
Your cues are confusing.
He was accused of abuse.
Are you used to using the computer?

Introducing the Sound

To make this sound, keep the mouth slightly open, with lips about ⅜ inch (1 cm) apart. (See Figure 7.)

The sound is short.

Figure 7.
The sound /ʌ/.

Listen to the following examples and repeat them after the speaker.

EXAMPLES

up	cousin	does
under	trouble	
	rough	was
love		
done	flood	
son	blood	

Practice for Mastery

Listen to the following sentences featuring the sound /ʌ/ and repeat them after the speaker.

EXAMPLES

> Buffy cut up the shrubs.
> The dust is under the rug.
> The mother won some of the money, but
> not enough.
> I'd love to come on Sunday if it's sunny.

Contrasting Sound Practice

To compare the /u/ from Unit Three with the sound /ʌ/, listen to the following words and repeat them after the speaker.

EXAMPLES

/u/	/ʌ/		/u/	/ʌ/
took	tuck		put	putt
look	luck		could	cud
book	buck			

Now listen to sentences that feature both vowel sounds, and repeat them after the speaker.

EXAMPLES

> Could you put a tuck in the front?
> Look at us for good luck.
> The bus looks good, but it's fun on foot.
> The hooded one looks tough.

Recognition Practice

Five words featuring these sounds are recorded on the tape. Circle below the words you hear. The correct answers are on page 21.

EXERCISE

1. look   luck
2. took   tuck
3. put   putt
4. could   cud
5. put   putt

Dictation Practice

Write the next five words recorded on the tape on a piece of paper, or repeat them during the pauses and write the exercise later. The correct answers appear below.

Spelling Challenge

Three sentences that have words with tricky spelling are next recorded on the tape. Listen to each one carefully, then write it down during the pause. Check your sentences below.

Answers to Exercises

Recognition Practice, luck, took, putt, could, put
Dictation Practice, luck, took, book, could, buck
Spelling Challenge, Stop rushing and pushing. The bus is busy. The poodle stood in a puddle of blood.

Introducing the Sound

To make this sound, lower your jaw slightly. The lips are tense and spread outward in a half-smile, about ½ inch (1.3 cm) apart. (See Figure 8.)

The sound is short.

Figure 8.
The sound /ɛ/.

Listen to the following examples and repeat them after the speaker.

EXAMPLES

egg	again	meadow	friend
edge	said	head	
step			heifer
	says	leopard	
any			guest
many			
can			bury

Practice for Mastery

Listen to the following sentences featuring the sound /ɛ/ and repeat them after the speaker.

22

EXAMPLES

Send Ben for his friend.
Let's rent a tent.
Esther never gets upset.
Fred said it again and again.

Contrasting Sound Practice

To compare the /ɪ/ sound from Unit Two with the sound /ɛ/, listen to the following words and repeat them after the speaker.

EXAMPLES

/ɪ/	/ɛ/	/ɪ/	/ɛ/
pick	peck	fill	fell
bid	bed	gym	gem
lid	led, lead	tin	ten
miss	mess	slipped	slept
wrist	rest	mitt	met
lift	left	six	sex
big	beg		

Now repeat the following sentences which feature both vowel sounds.

EXAMPLES

Pick a peck of pickled peppers.
Ed slipped and fell in the gym.
Evelyn missed the best bid.
Peg slept from six 'til ten, then left.

Recognition Practice

Five words featuring these sounds are recorded on the tape. Circle below the words you hear, then check them on page 25.

EXERCISE

1. lid	led
2. big	beg
3. slipped	slept
4. gym	gem
5. lift	left

Dictation Practice

Five words that contain these sounds are recorded on the tape. Write them during the pauses, then check them on page 25. If you have several errors, practice Units Two and Eight again.

If you do not hear the difference between the two vowel sounds, do not be discouraged. By making the sounds correctly, putting your lips and jaw in the positions described, you will begin to hear the difference.

Spelling Challenge

Three sentences containing words with tricky spelling are recorded next on the tape. During the pauses, write them down on a piece of paper. Check them on page 25.

Now compare /iy/ from Unit Four with the sound /ɛ/. Listen to the examples and repeat them after the speaker.

EXAMPLES

/iy/	/ɛ/	/iy/	/ɛ/
beat, beet	bet	read, reed	red, read
feel	fell	seed	said
geese	guess	sealing, ceiling	selling
he'd, heed	head	sees	says
mean	men	bleed	bled

Listen to several sentences that feature these two sounds, and repeat them after the speaker.

EXAMPLES

Please feed the pets and weed the beds.
He said he'd eat the red meat.
She says she fell and she's bleeding.
Steve guessed he'd been seen in the shed.

Recognition Practice

Five words featuring these sounds are recorded next on the tape. Circle below the ones you hear. The correct answers appear below.

EXERCISE

1. teen   ten
2. mean   men
3. heed   head
4. seal   sell
5. geese   guess

Dictation Practice

Now the speaker will pronounce five words featuring these sounds. Write the words on a piece of paper, then check your answers with the list below.

Answers to Exercises

Recognition Practice, p. 24 lid, big, slept, gem, left
Dictation Practice, p. 24 tin, miss, pick, bed, six
Spelling Challenge, The queen has been seen. He's the truest guest. Betty is pretty already.
Recognition Practice, ten, mean, head, seal, geese
Dictation Practice, said, wrecks, feel, he'd or heed, guess

Introducing the Sound

To pronounce /ow/, with your lips about ½ inch (1.3 cm) apart, round them into a circle. Begin the sound, then move your lips into a smaller circle. (See Figure 9.)

The sound is long.

Figure 9.
The sound /ow/.

Listen to the examples and repeat them after the speaker.

EXAMPLES

over	yeoman	groan	mauve
go			faux
zero	oh	sew	
			brooch
	depot	soul	
plateau		shoulder	
	though		
owner			
slow	hoe		
window			

Practice for Mastery

Listen to the following sentences featuring the sound /ow/ and repeat them after the speaker.

EXAMPLES

> Oh no, don't go!
> Show Joe the snowmobile.
> Flo chose to row the old boat.
> Throw your stole over your shoulder.

The /ow/ followed by the consonant /r/ is slightly different. When rounding your lips, push them outward, away from the top teeth, making the /r/ sound.

Listen to the examples and repeat them after the speaker.

EXAMPLES

or	four	soar
for	pour	board
wore		
	poor	toward
war	door	drawer
warm		

Practice for Mastery

Listen to the following sentences featuring the sound /or/, and repeat them after the speaker.

EXAMPLES

> Your war stories are boring.
> He wore shorts to the store.
> Pour four more quarts.
> Morton's court report was short.

Contrasting Sound Practice

Now compare /ʌ/ from Unit Seven, with /ow/. Listen to the words and repeat them after the speaker.

EXAMPLES

/ʌ/	/ow/	/ʌ/	/ow/
fun	phone	shun	shone
rum	roam	rub	robe
dove	dove	mud	mode, mowed
come	comb	rug	rogue
hum	home	cup	cope
crumb	chrome	nut	note

Now say the following sentences.

EXAMPLES

Bud wrote one note home.
Rose coped with the crumbs.
Lola rubbed the mud from the old rug.
Phone him at home just for fun.

Recognition Practice

The speaker will pronounce five words containing these sounds. Circle the words you hear, or repeat them now, and do the written exercise later. The answers are on page 29.

EXERCISE

1. cup	cope
2. come	comb
3. nut	note
4. fun	phone
5. shun	shone

Dictation Practice

Now write the next five words recorded on the tape on a piece of paper. Check your answers below.

Spelling Challenge

Ten sentences containing words with confusing spelling are recorded next on the tape. Write them down on a piece of paper during the pauses, then check your work below.

Answers to Exercises

Recognition Practice, p. 28 cup, comb, nut, phone, shone
Dictation Practice, p. 29 rug, note, cup, coat, home
Spelling Challenge, Whose shoes are those? Whose hose did you lose? So, sew a few new suits. Move it above the stove. Go do it. Come home. The mover put a cover over the oven. Does she have toes in her shoes? Worms have many forms. Work with the fork.

Introducing the Sound

The /oiy/ sound is a combination of two sounds beginning with /o/ and ending in /iy/. The lips, set about ½ inch (1.3 cm) apart, begin in a circle. (See Figure 10.) The sound ends with the lips in a wide smile, and ⅜ inch (1 cm) apart.

The sound is long.

Figure 10.
The sound /oiy/.

Listen to the examples and repeat them after the speaker.

EXAMPLES

boy	boil	poise
toy	soil	noisy
	coin	

Practice for Mastery

Listen to the following sentences featuring the sound /oiy/, and repeat them after the speaker.

EXAMPLES

Roy's toys are noisy.
The boy pointed to the poison.
Troy's ploy was foiled.
The spoiled boy destroyed Floyd's joy.

Introducing the Sound

To make this sound, keep your jaw halfway open. The lips are ½ inch (1.3 cm) apart. Tense your lips, and form a wide, downward smile. Begin the sound, then move your lips close together into the /ə/ position. (See Figure 11.)

The sound is long.

Figure 11.
The sound /eə/.

Listen to the examples and repeat them after the speaker.

EXAMPLES

ran	laugh
fast	
pass	
craft	

To pronounce the vowel /eə/ followed by the consonant /r/, begin with the /eə/ sound, then move the lips forward into a round shape, baring the front teeth

32

As before, listen to the examples and repeat them after the speaker.

EXAMPLES

care	wear	fair	where
dare	bear	stairs	there
	aerial	heir	they're
		their	
		prayer	

Practice for Mastery

Repeat the following sentences after the speaker

EXAMPLES

The fair-haired man ran in the sand.
Where are the spare pairs Stan and Dan wear?
They're not your socks. They're theirs.
Frances laughed when she passed him on
the stairs.
They're cramming for their exams over there.

Contrasting Sound Practice

Compare /iy/, from Unit Four, with /eə/ by repeating the following words.

EXAMPLES

/iy/	/eə/
leaf	laugh
mean	man
clean	clan
fiend	fanned
peace, piece	pass
leaned	land

/iy/	/eə/
we're	where, wear
beer	bear
cheer	chair
peer	pear, pair, pare
steer	stair, stare
fear	fair, fare
here, hear	hair, hare
ear	air
tear, tier	tear

Now say these sentences, which feature both vowel sounds.

EXAMPLES

> Sheila ran past the stairs with a can of beer.
> The lean man cheered and laughed.
> She can't eat peas from a can.
> We're in need of a tank of gas.

Recognition Practice

The speaker will pronounce five words. Circle the ones you hear, or repeat the words and do the written exercise later. The answers are on page 36.

EXERCISE

1. peace   pass
2. here   hair
3. we're   where
4. leaned   land
5. ear   air

Dictation Practice

Write the next five words recorded on the tape on a piece of paper, then check your work on page 36.

Contrasting Sound Practice

To compare /ɛ/ from Unit Eight with /eə/, repeat the following words after the speaker.

EXAMPLES

/ɛ/	/eə/		/ɛ/	/eə/
lend	land		men	man
left	laughed		messed	mast
pen	pan		guess	gas
wren	ran			

Now repeat several sentences that feature these sounds.

EXAMPLES

The man laughed, then left.
I guess Ann and Ed ran out of gas.
Fran passed the pen to the man's left hand.
Can Ted send a letter to Stan?

Recognition Practice

Listen to the next five words recorded on the tape and circle the ones you hear. The answers are on page 36.

EXERCISE

1. men   man
2. pen   pan
3. wren   ran
4. lend   land
5. guess   gas

Dictation Practice

Write the next five words recorded on the tape on a piece of paper. When you finish, check your answers with the list below.

Spelling Challenge

Now write the next three sentences you hear recorded on the tape.

Check your work below.

Answers to Exercises

Recognition Practice, p. 34 pass, here, we're, land, ear
Dictation Practice, p. 35 we're, mean, steer, laugh, man
Recognition Practice, p. 35 men, pan, ran, lend, gas
Dictation Practice, laughed, guess, man, messed, pen
Spelling Challenge, There were three people here. Where were you? I can can the tomatoes.

Introducing the Sound

This is a combination of sounds. Begin with your lips in the first position of /eə/, about ½ inch (1.3 cm) apart and with a wide, downward smile. Then, slowly widen them into an upward smile, forming /iy/. (See Figure 12.)

Count to two silently to be sure the sound is long enough.

Figure 12.
The sound /eiy/.

Listen to the examples and repeat them after the speaker.

EXAMPLES

ate	cafe	prey	**eight**
face		they	rein
	gauge		
day		ballet	great
way	pain		
		suede	
	straight		
		fiancee	

Move your lips into the /ə/ position after /eiy/ when it occurs before the consonant /l/.

Listen to the examples and repeat them after the speaker.

EXAMPLES

pale	sail	they'll

Practice for Mastery

Repeat the following sentences which feature the sound /eiy/.

EXAMPLES

> It rained eight days.
> The suede cape has a great shape.
> Renee ate creme brulee at the buffet today.
> The rain in Spain stays mainly in the plain.
> She laid the frail lace on the table.

Contrasting Sound Practice

To compare the sound /ɛ/, from Unit Eight, with /eiy/, repeat the following words.

EXAMPLES

lɛl	*leiyl*		*lɛl*	*leiyl*
red	raid		pen	pane, pain
bet	bait		wren	rain, rein, reign
debt	date		test	taste
fell	fail		shed	shade
get	gate		tent	taint
mess	mace			

Now repeat several sentences that feature both sounds.

EXAMPLES

> Fred's cake failed the taste test.
> Get the red dress for your date.
> Jane's friend fell on the train.
> Sell ten shares and trade the rest.

Recognition Practice

Five words featuring the sounds /ɛ/ and /**eiy**/ are recorded next on the tape. Circle below the words you hear, then check them below.

EXERCISE

1. pen	pain
2. test	taste
3. debt	date
4. fell	fail
5. get	gate

Dictation Practice

Five words containing these sounds are recorded next on the tape. Write them on a piece of paper during the pauses, then check them below.

Spelling Challenge

Seven sentences containing words with confusing spelling are recorded next on the tape. Listen to them carefully and write them down on a piece of paper during the pauses. Check them below.

Answers to Exercises

Recognition Practice, pain, test, debt, fail, get
Dictation Practice, red, bait, shade, fell, mess
Spelling Challenge, The pain came again. Her friend is a fiend for french fries. There were many zany women. The ape ate eight apples and an apricot. Hey, where's the key? She said she was afraid. The players said their prayers and paid their debts.

Introducing the Sound

To make the vowel sound /ɔ/, drop your jaw until the lips are ⅝ inch (1.5 cm) apart. Tense your lips and round them forward halfway. (See Figure 13.)

The sound is long.

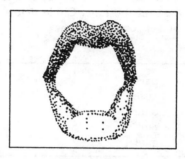

Figure 13.
The sound /ɔ/.

Listen to the examples and repeat them after the speaker.

EXAMPLES

off	all	daughter	cough
on	call	caught	bought
often			
	auto	awful	broad
	fault	lawn	

Practice for Mastery

Listen to the following sentences featuring the sound /ɔ/, and repeat them after the speaker.

EXAMPLES

> Draw water from the faucet.
> The water is always calm in August.
> I thought Audrey saw a lawyer.
> You ought to have brought your daughter.

Contrasting Sound Practice

To compare /ʌ/, from Unit Seven, with /ɔ/, repeat these words after the speaker.

EXAMPLES

/ʌ/	/ɔ/	/ʌ/	/ɔ/
cuff	cough	sung	song
gun	gone	rung	wrong
but	bought	cut	caught
lung	long	gulf	golf

Now, say the next sentences after the speaker.

EXAMPLES

> Bud was caught with the gun he bought.
> Sunny has sung all the wrong love songs.
> Audrey bought the awesome puppies.
> Maud cut the cuffs from that awful cloth.

Recognition Practice

Listen to the next five words recorded on the tape, and circle below the ones you hear. The answers are on page 43.

EXERCISE

1. lung   long
2. cut   caught
3. gun   gone
4. cut   caught
5. gulf   golf

Dictation Practice

Now write the next five words recorded on the tape on a piece of paper, then check your answers on page 43.

Contrasting Sound Practice

To compare /ow/, from Unit Nine, with /ɔ/, repeat the following words.

EXAMPLES

/ow/	/ɔ/	/ow/	/ɔ/
loan	lawn	loafed	loft
boat	bought	bowl	ball
coat	caught	own	on
oaf	off	boast	bossed

Now say these sentences after the speaker.

EXAMPLES

Joe caught the mole in his lawn.
Paula lost her coat on the long walk.
The tall author is his own boss.
He bought the old boat, then walked home.

Recognition Practice

Listen to the next five words recorded on the tape, and circle the ones you hear. Check your answers below.

EXERCISE

1. loafed	loft
2. coat	caught
3. bowl	ball
4. boast	bossed
5. loan	lawn

Dictation Practice

Now write the five words recorded next on the tape on a piece of paper. Check your answers below.

Spelling Challenge

Write the four sentences recorded on the tape during the pauses, then check them below.

Answers to Exercises

Recognition Practice, p. 42 lung, cut, gone, caught, golf
Dictation Practice, p. 42 song, but, gulf, cough, cuff
Recognition Practice, loafed, caught, bowl, boast, lawn
Dictation Practice, off, own, coat, bought, loaf
Spelling Challenge, The wolf plays golf. He laughed when he was caught with the faux diamond. Although the rough cough went through him, he was tough. She has gone and done it alone.

Introducing the Sound

To make this sound, keep your lips ⅝ inch (1.5 cm) apart and form a half-smile, with tense lips. (See Figure 14.)

The sound is short.

Figure 14.
The sound /æ/.

Listen to the examples and repeat them after the speaker.

EXAMPLES

back	plaid	meringue
cat		
tap		
bag		
pad		
cab		

Practice for Mastery

Listen to the following sentences featuring the sound /æ/, and repeat them after the speaker.

AMPLES

> Pack the bags.
> Have *a* snack, Jack.
> Pat's cat is fat.
> Her plaid jacket has black snaps.

ontrasting Sound Practice

To compare /iy/, from Unit Four, with /æ/,)eat the following words after the speaker.

AMPLES

iy/	/æ/	/iy/	/æ/
eet, feat	fat	heed, he'd	had
eat	sat	he's	has
eed	sad	heat	hat
eap	lap	neat	gnat

Now repeat these sentences.

MPLES

> 'lease feed the cats.
> Ie needs *a* black hat.
> Matt has *a* shack near the sea.
> he believes that Pete has had *a* nap.

cognition Practice

ive words featuring these sounds are recorded
t on the tape. Below, circle the ones you hear,
n check the answers on page 47.

EXERCISE

1. feet	fat
2. leap	lap
3. he'd	had
4. seed	sad
5. heat	hat

Dictation Practice

Write the next five words recorded on the tape o
a piece of paper. When you finish, check your wo
on page 47.

Contrasting Sound Practice

Compare the /ɛ/ of Unit Eight with /æ/
repeating each word after the speaker.

EXAMPLES

/ɛ/	/æ/	/ɛ/	/æ/
beg	bag	wreck	rack
head	had	set	sat
met	mat	said	sad
pet	pat	pled	plaid

Listen to the following sentences that feature /
and /æ/, and repeat them after the speaker.

EXAMPLES

The pet cat sat on the bed.
Pat had a red rag on her head.
The men said it had a sad ending.
The next guest patted Fred on the back.

Recognition Practice

Five words featuring these sounds are recorded next on the tape. Circle them below, then check them below.

EXERCISE

1. met	mat
2. set	sat
3. wreck	rack
4. head	had
5. said	sad

Dictation Practice

Write the next five words recorded on the tape on a piece of paper. When you finish, check your words below.

Answers to Exercises

Recognition Practice, p. 46 fat, leap, he'd, sad, heat
Dictation Practice, p. 46 sad, has, he's, seed, feet or feat
Recognition Practice, mat, set, wreck, had, sad
Dictation Practice, head, pet, said, rack, beg

Introducing the Sound

This is a combination of vowel sounds. Begin wi
/æ/ by setting your lips ⅝ inch (1.5 cm) apart; the
glide into /ow/, forming a circle with your lips. (S
Figure 15.)

The sound is long.

Figure 15.
The sound /æow/.

Listen to the examples and repeat them after tł
speaker.

EXAMPLES

how	house	**bough**
now	*a*loud	
brown		

To pronounce /æow/ before the consonant /r
begin with /æow/, move your lips to the /ə/ po:
tion, then round them and push them outward in
the /r/ position. This is a very long vowel sound.

Repeat the examples of the sound /æowər/.

EXAMPLES

sour	sauerkraut	power
flour		
hour		

Practice for Mastery

Now, repeat the following sentences featuring the sound /æow/.

EXAMPLES

Our townh**ou**se has *a* br**ow**n m**ou**se.
Are we all**ow**ed t**o** speak al**ou**d?
We f**ou**nd **our** g**ow**ns d**ow**nt**ow**n.
Sh**ow**er the fl**ow**ers for *a*n h**ou**r.
H**ow**'s the s**au**erkraut?

Spelling Challenge

The next nine sentences, which contain words with tricky spelling, are recorded on the tape. Write them during the pauses, then check your work below.

Answers to Exercise

Spelling Challenge, Ouch! Don't touch me. You found out you could wound him. She wound the bandage around the wound. Slow down now. It's snowing. The rouge covered the gouge. It's my own gown. Of course the mouse couldn't eat the mousse, but my cousin could. He's the flower grower. On a tour of the mill, we bought four bags of flour.

Introducing the Sound

To make this sound, drop your jaw until the lips are about ¾ inch (2 cm) apart, but relaxed. (See Figure 16.)

The sound is short but takes a little longer because your mouth is open so wide!

Figure 16.
The sound /a/.

Listen to the examples and repeat them after the speaker.

EXAMPLES

father	cot	honor	knowledge
wand	doll	honest	
	lock		bureaucracy
	option	encore	
		ennui	

Practice for Mastery

Listen to the following sentences featuring the sound /a/, and repeat them after the speaker.

EXAMPLES

> Roz is fond of dolls.
> John got an honest job.
> Bob stopped in the shop for a mop.
> His knowledge of crops is obvious.

Contrasting Sound Practice

Compare /ʌ/, from Unit Seven, with /a/. Repeat these words after the speaker.

EXAMPLES

/ʌ/	/a/	/ʌ/	/a/
hut	hot	shut	shot
buddy	body	putt	pot
cup	cop	gut	got
rut	rot	nut	not, knot

Now, say the following sentences.

EXAMPLES

> Her brother got a hot supper.
> Some shots are optional.
> Buddy dropped the hot cup in the shop.
> Stop fussing and come up.

Recognition Practice

Five words featuring these sounds are recorded next on the tape. Circle below the ones you hear, then check them on page 53.

Exercise

1. buddy	body
2. hut	hot
3. shut	shot
4. hut	hot
5. nut	not

Dictation Practice

Listen to the next five words on the tape and write them on a piece of paper during the pauses. Check them on page 53 when you finish.

The /a/ when followed by /r/, ends with the lips pushed outward; this changes the sound somewhat.

Listen to the examples and repeat them after the speaker, then listen for the confirmation.

Examples

arm	bazaar	guard	sergeant
ark			
far			heart
carve			

Practice for Mastery

Listen to the following sentences, which contain the /a/ sound followed by /r/, and repeat them after the speaker.

Examples

Are the stars far from Mars?
The hard part is to start the car.
Sergeant Barton was the guard.
He carved a large heart in the bark.

Spelling Challenge

During the pauses, write the next six sentences you hear on the tape. Check your work below.

Answers to Exercises

Recognition Practice, p. 52 body, hut, shut, hot, nut
Dictation Practice, p. 52 cop, shot, buddy, cup, knot or not
Spelling Challenge, We're here to honor the donor. Don't bother my brother or my father. They found a comb and a bomb in the tomb. Ron's son won the ribbon. Please polish the Polish medal. It's warm on the farm.

Introducing the Sound

The /**aiy**/ sound is a double vowel. Begin sounding the /**a**/, with the lips about ¾ inch (2 cm) apart. Then move your lips to the /**iy**/ position, forming a big smile. (See Figure 17.)

This is a long sound.

Figure 17.
The sound /aiy/.

Listen to the examples, repeat them after the speaker, then listen for the confirmation.

EXAMPLES

I	pie	aisle	my
I'd	dried		fly
		height	
ice	might		guy
bike			buy

Practice for Mastery

Listen to the following sentences featuring the sound /**aiy**/, and repeat them after the speaker.

EXAMPLES

> Ida buys nice surprises.
> I'm twice your size, Liza!
> Try my pie, Ira!
> That guy might buy my cycle.

Spelling Challenge

During the pauses, write the next three sentences you hear on the tape, then check your work below.

Answers to Exercise

Spelling Challenge, Write down your height and weight. The police officers are nice and polite. I find that the wind bothers my brother.

PART TWO
ENGLISH CONSONANT Sounds

Consonant sounds are determined by
- the position of the tongue, lips, and teeth
- the way air is released
- the use of, or absence of, voice

Study Figure 18, then follow the directions for each sound.

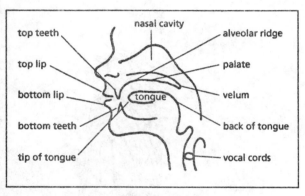

Figure 18.

Introducing the Sound /p/

To make the sound /p/, put your lips together firmly, stop the air completely, then pop the lips open. Do not make a vocal sound. (See Figure 19.)

At the beginning of words, release /p/ with a puff of air. To be sure the puff of air is strong enough, place a small piece of paper in front of your mouth when pronouncing the following words. The paper should move considerably.

Figure 19.
The sound /p/.

Listen to the following examples and repeat them after the speaker.

Examples

pay	**p**it	**p**lay
pat	**p**ot	**p**raise
peck		

Make the same puff of air when a word ends in another consonant plus /p/.

Listen to the following examples and repeat them after the speaker.

EXAMPLES

lam**p**	har**p**	gras**p**
lim**p**	shar**p**	was**p**

Do not make the puff of air when /**p**/ occurs in the middle of a word before a vowel sound.

Listen to the following examples and repeat them after the speaker.

EXAMPLES

ap**p**le	sim**p**le	pur**p**le
ha**pp**y	peo**p**le	

Do not make the puff of air when /**p**/ directly follows the sound /s/ at the beginning or in the middle of a word.

Listen to the examples and repeat them after the speaker.

EXAMPLES

s**p**an	whis**p**er
s**p**end	hos**p**ital
s**p**ill	as**p**irin
s**p**oil	ex**p**ect

When /**p**/ is the last sound in a word and is followed by another word, do not pop your lips open. Bring the lips together firmly, making no vocal sound, then say the next word.

Listen to the following sentences and repeat them after the speaker.

EXAMPLES

> Put the top down.
> Keep trying.
> I hope to stop them.
> It's up there.
> The map you gave me is helpful.

When /p/ is the last sound, make it either with or without the puff of air. There is no difference in meaning.

Listen to the following examples of sentences read both ways and repeat them after the speaker.

EXAMPLES

With the puff	**Without the puff**
Stop!	Stop!
Read the map.	Read the map.
Let's go on *a* trip.	Let's go on *a* trip.
I need some sleep.	I need some sleep.
Never give up.	Never give up.

Practice for Mastery

Listen to the following sentences featuring the sound /p/, and repeat them after the speaker.

EXAMPLES

> Please prepare the pizza for the party.
> Pat helped me pick up the papers.
> Put the stamps on the package.
> Mr. Bishop paid for the lamp in April.
> Phillip didn't give me *a* map.
> Penny has the hiccoughs.

About the Letter p

The letter p followed by the letter h is usually pronounced /f/.

The letter p is silent (not pronounced) in the following words. Listen, and repeat each word after the speaker.

EXAMPLES

receipt	corps	cupboard
psychology	raspberry	sapphire
pneumonia		

Introducing the Sound /b/

To pronounce /b/, place your lips together firmly; stop the air completely, and make a voiced sound. (See Figure 20.)

Figure 20.
The sound /b/.

Listen to the following examples and repeat them after the speaker.

EXAMPLES

bag	rubber
bread	sobbed
bulb	
observe	
cabs	

Practice for Mastery

Listen to the following sentences featuring the sound /b/, and repeat them after the speaker.

EXAMPLES

Billy grabbed the sobbing baby.
The bushes and bulbs are about to bloom.
Bob was bleeding, and his bones were broken.
Maybe Elizabeth brags a bit.

About the Letter b

The letter b is silent in the following words. Listen, and repeat each word after the speaker.

EXAMPLES

debt	comb	subtle
doubt	tomb	subpoena
lamb	womb	

Contrasting Sound Practice

Compare the sound /p/ with the sound /b/ by repeating the following words after the speaker.

Examples

/p/	/b/
pin	bin
pet	bet
pack	back
pole	bowl
push	bush
pour, pore	bore, boar
punch	bunch
prayed	braid
repel	rebel
rapid	rabid
roped	robed
ripped	ribbed
pare, pair, pear	bare, bear

Recognition Practice

Listen to the next four sentences recorded on the tape. Circle the ones you hear, or repeat the sentences now and do the written exercise later. The correct answers are below.

Exercise

1. I can't pare it.	I can't bear it.
2. Paul needs a push in front of his house.	Paul needs a bush in front of his house.
3. We bought a big pole.	We bought a big bowl.
4. Patty has some new cups.	Patty has some new cubs.

Answers to Exercise

Recognition Practice, I can't bear it. Paul needs a push in front of his house. We bought a big pole. Patty has some new cubs.

Introducing the Sound /t/

Place the tip of the tongue against the alveolar ridge, stop the air completely, then release the air. (See Figure 21.) Do not make a vocal sound.

There are several variations of this consonant.

Figure 21.
The sound /t/.

When a word begins with /t/, make the sound with a noisy puff of air.

To be sure the puff of air is noisy enough, hold a small piece of paper in front of your mouth when pronouncing the following words. It should move considerably.

Listen to the following examples and repeat them after the speaker.

EXAMPLES

tame	ten	tray	thyme
tap	tip	tree	
team		twin	
		twelve	

65

Make the same noisy puff when a word ends in another consonant sound plus /t/.

Listen to the examples and repeat them after the speaker.

EXAMPLES

act	apt
lift	last
fault	borscht
can't	text

Usage Tips

- Make the same noisy puff for **-st** or **-est** at the end of an adjective to make the superlative form.

Listen to the examples and repeat them after the speaker.

EXAMPLES

best	worst	most
biggest	smallest	least
happiest	silliest	

- The past tense marker, **ed**, is pronounced /t/, with the puff of air, when the verb ends in a voiceless consonant sound such as /p/, /k/, /ch/, /f/, /sh/, /s/, or /ks/. Be careful not to make a vowel sound before the /t/.

Listen to the examples and repeat them after the speaker.

EXAMPLES

taped	washed
picked	passed
watched	faxed
laughed	

Do not make the puff of air when /t/ follows /s/ at the beginning of a syllable.

EXAMPLES

stamp	mistake
step	faster
stove	history

• To pronounce /t/ just before the sound /s/ at the end of words, tap the tip of your tongue on the palate, then slide your tongue forward to make /s/.

Listen to the examples and repeat them after the speaker.

EXAMPLES

bats	cats
rests	beasts
bites	coats

To produce the /t/ at the end of words that occur before words beginning with a consonant, tap your tongue on the alveolar ridge, stop the vocal sound, then go on to the next word.

Listen to the examples and repeat them after the speaker.

EXAMPLES

She ate three hotdogs.
The fat cat sat down on the mat.
I'll bet she got the hat with that money.
I met them at the market.

In certain words, the /t/ is unreleased as above, then followed by the sound /n/.

Listen to the examples and repeat them after the speaker.

EXAMPLES

button	fountain	important
mitten	mountain	sentence
kitten		
bitten		

When the last word you say ends in the sound /t/, pronounce it either with or without the puff of air. There is no difference in meaning.

Listen to the following sentences read both ways, and repeat them after the speaker.

EXAMPLES

With the puff	**Without the puff**
He sat on his hat.	He sat on his hat.
She put on her coat.	She put on her coat.
They came to visit.	They came to visit.
He didn't eat.	He didn't eat.
I didn't say that.	I didn't say that.

Practice for Mastery

Listen to the following sentences featuring the sound /t/, and repeat them after the speaker.

EXAMPLES

Those tenants tore up the apartment.
Leave the stew on the stove for two minutes.
Just a minute, please.
I put the buttons in my pocket.
Stand up straight.
Janet washed her skirt and two t-shirts.
She wished she had polished her boots.
The last time I went to that store, I got lost.

About the Letter t

The letter t, when followed by the sound /iuw/ is usually pronounced /ch/ (See Unit Twenty-two, page 88.)

When the letter t occurs between vowels, it has one of the pronunciations of the sound /d/. (See Introducing the Sound /d/, which follows.)

The letter t is silent in the following words. Listen, and repeat each word after the speaker.

EXAMPLES

often	fasten	mortgage
listen	hasten	mustn't

See Unit Twenty-nine for the pronunciation of the letter t followed by h.

Introducing the Sound /d/

To make the sound /d/ place the tip of the tongue on the alveolar ridge and make a voiced sound. (See Figure 22.)

Figure 22.
The sound /d/.

Hold the /d/ slightly at the beginning of a word, then release it with the next sound.

Listen to the examples and repeat them after the speaker.

EXAMPLES

day	**d**ress	**d**warf
dime	**d**rive	
does		
doll*a*r		
do		

At the end of words, before consonants, hold your tongue briefly on the alveolar ridge, then go on to the next word.

Listen to the examples and repeat them after the speaker.

EXAMPLES

Tell da**d** to drive.
Th*e* be**d** belongs to me.
Th*e* li**d** fell off.
When **d**oes th*e* ti**d**e come in?
Th*e* co**d**e number *is* on th*e* back.

To make the sound of /d/ between vowels and after the consonant /r/, tap the tongue quickly on the palate without holding it, then go on to the next vowel.

Note that this sound is often spelled with the letter t̲.

Listen to the examples and repeat them after the speaker

EXAMPLES

la**d**y	city	sub**t**le
bo**d**y	la**t**er	
fa**d**ed	shor**t**er	li**tt**le
gra**d**ed	gra**t**ed	
har**d**er		
or**d**er		

Usage Tips

• To make the regular past tense, add /d/ to verbs that end in a vowel sound or one of the voiced consonants — /b/, /g/, /v/, /j/, /l/, /m/, /n/, /r/, /z/, /w/, or /y/. Do not make a vowel sound before the /d/.

Listen to the examples and repeat them after the speaker.

EXAMPLES

playe**d**	rubbe**d**	hemme**d**
staye**d**	hugge**d**	canne**d**
crie**d**	love**d**	feare**d**
snowe**d**	judge**d**	buzze**d**
glue**d**	rolle**d**	

• Add the unstressed vowel /ə/ plus /d/ to verbs ending with the sound /d/ or /t/. The verb now has one more syllable.

Listen to the examples and repeat them after the speaker.

EXAMPLES

fad**ed**	want**ed**
end**ed**	plant**ed**
land**ed**	invit**ed**
fold**ed**	creat**ed**
load**ed**	greet**ed**

• A pronoun plus '/d/ forms a contraction for the modals <u>had</u> and <u>would</u>.

Listen to the examples and repeat them after the speaker.

EXAMPLES

I'**d** been there be*f*ore.	(I had been there before.)
They'**d** called us earli*er*.	(They had called us earlier.)
We'**d** better stay.	(We had better stay.)
You'**d** better not do that.	(You had better not do that.)
I'**d** help you *if* I could.	(I would help you if I could.)
He'**d** come *if* he want*e*d to.	(He would come if he wanted to.)
We'**d** like *a* drink.	(We would like a drink.)

Practice for Mastery

Listen to the following sentences featuring the sound /**d**/, and repeat them after the speaker.

EXAMPLES

Dan **d**rove us *a*roun**d** be*f*ore **d**inner.
Does **D**onn*a* have *a* **d**oll*ar*?
Davi**d** di**d**n't **d**o th*e* **d**ish*es*.

He sai**d** it.
I got it.
She di**d** it.

That be**d** is ol**d**.
She ha**d** *a* ba**d** col**d**.
He ate *a* bit *of* but**t**er.

Fre**d** *is a* forty-year-ol**d** veteran.
Pa**tt**y sat on the li**tt**le la**dd**er.
E**dd**y's thirty to**d**ay.
It's *a* beau**t**iful city, b**u**t it's so dirty!

About the Letter **d**

The letter **d** followed by the sound /**iuw**/ is usually pronounced /**j**/. (See Unit Twenty-two, page 88.)

The letter **d** is silent in the following words. Listen, and repeat each word after the speaker.

EXAMPLES

Wednesday
grandfather
grandmother
grandchildren
handkerchief

Practice in Context

Listen to the following poem featuring the final past tense sounds /t/, /d/, and /əd/, and repeat each line after the speaker.

The Surprise Party

/t/
They shopped, spent, cooked, ate,
Drank, gossiped, laughed, baked,
Stopped and talked,
Worked and walked.

/d/
They planned, saved, sewed, schemed,
Programmed, whispered, giggled, dreamed,
Enjoyed and played,
A party made.
/əd/
They decorated and waited,
Then shouted and celebrated.

Now listen to a tongue twister that features the
sounds /t/ and /d/, and repeat each line after the
speaker.

The Tutor

A tutor who tooted the flute
Tried to teach two young tooters to toot,
Said the two to the tutor:
"Is it harder to toot,
or to tutor two tooters to toot?"

Introducing the Sound /k/

To pronounce /k/, bring the back of the tongue to the velum, stop the air completely, then release it with a voiceless sound. (See Figure 23.)

Figure 23.
The sound /k/.

At the beginning of words, release /k/ with a puff of air. To make sure the puff of air is strong enough, hold a small piece of paper in front of your mouth as you say the following words. The paper should move considerably.

Listen to the following examples, and repeat them after the speaker.

EXAMPLES

cat	clean	kettle
cost	crazy	
		khaki

Make the same puff of air when a word ends in another consonant plus /k/.

Listen to the following examples, and repeat them after the speaker.

Examples

frank	work	as**k**	tal**k**
in**k**	for**k**		wal**k**
		mos**q**ue	

Do not make the puff of air when /k/ is followed by the sound /w/.

Listen to the examples and repeat them after the speaker.

Examples

quick
queen
question
quite

Do not make the puff when /k/ occurs in the middle of a word before a vowel sound.

Listen to the following examples, and repeat them after the speaker.

Examples

lan**k**y	sti**ck**y	un**cl**e	la**cqu**er
as**k**ing	ti**ckl**e	cho**c**olate	
mon**k**ey	wi**ck**ed		sa**cc**harine

When /k/ occurs just after the sound /s/, there is no puff of air.

Listen to the following examples, and repeat them after the speaker.

EXAMPLES

skin	school
skate	schedule
basket	
scrape	

When /k/ occurs just before another consonant, bring the back of the tongue to the velum, stop the air briefly, but do not release it; then make the next sound.

Listen to the examples, and repeat them after the speaker.

EXAMPLES

asks	asked	action
likes	liked	actor
bakes	baked	picture
		anxious

Listen to the following sentences, and repeat them after the speaker.

EXAMPLES

Pick the music up tomorrow.
Look at the black bike over there.
I'll make a cake in the morning.
Did Rick rake the leaves?
Luke fell off his bike and scraped his skin.

When /k/ is the last sound in a word or sentence, pronounce it with or without the puff of air. There is no difference in meaning.

Listen to the following examples of sentences read both ways and repeat them after the speaker.

EXAMPLES

With the puff	Without the puff
Don't look!	Don't look!
That's *a* fake.	That's *a* fake.
I have a stoma**ch** a**ch**e.	I have a stoma**ch** a**ch**e.

Practice for Mastery

Listen to the following sentences featuring the sound /**k**/, and repeat them after the speaker.

EXAMPLES

Can you **c**ut the **c**ake for me?
Caroly**n** **c**ouldn't **c**ome to the **c**oncert.
His wi**ck**ed un**cl**e has no s**cr**uples.
Mi**k**e and Ja**ck** **c**an wor**k** **qu**i**ck**ly.
He wal**k**s to the ban**k** every day.
They tal**k**ed and as**k**ed **qu**estions.

About the Letters **k** and **c**

The letter **k** is not pronounced in the following words. Listen, and repeat each word after the speaker.

EXAMPLES

know	knowledge	knife
knew	knee	blackguard

The letter **c** is silent in the following word. Listen, and repeat after the speaker.

EXAMPLE

indict

Introducing the Sound /g/

To make the sound /g/, bring the back of the tongue to the velum, stop the air briefly, then release it with a voiced sound. (See Figure 24.)

Figure 24.
The sound /g/.

Listen to the examples and repeat them after the speaker.

EXAMPLES

game	egg	**gh**ost
glad	eggs	
grade	bigger	
	rugged	

Practice for Mastery

Listen to the following sentences featuring the sound /g/, and repeat them after the speaker.

EXAMPLES

> Go get your grandmother's glasses.
> Peggy begged to go to the art gallery.
> Gloria gives gracious get-togethers.
> Please give me eight gallons of gas.
> Maggie bagged all the groceries.
> Gayle dragged the rugged luggage through
> the gate.

Contrasting Sound Practice

To compare /g/ with /k/, repeat the following words after the speaker.

EXAMPLES

/k/	/g/	/k/	/g/
cot	got	back	bag
cane	gain	pick	pig
came	game	hawk	hog
come	gum	bicker	bigger
clean	glean	sacked	sagged
curl	girl	tacked, tact	tagged
rack	rag		

Recognition Practice

The speaker will read four sentences. Circle the ones you hear, or repeat them during the pauses and do the written exercise later. The answers are on page 81.

EXERCISE

1. Gary got a clean rag.   Gary got a clean rack.
2. He is just like a hawk.   He is just like a hog.
3. We need the glue.   We need the clue.
4. Please put it in   Please put it in
   the back.   the bag.

About the Letter g

The letter g after the letter n̲ has the sound /ŋ/.
See Unit Twenty-six, page 114.

The letter g is not pronounced in the following
words. Listen, and repeat each word after the speaker.

EXAMPLES

phlegm	caught, taught	weight, eight
diaphragm	bought, brought	might, light
sign	through	campaign
champagne	though	reign
lasagna	height	

Answers to Exercise

Recognition Practice, p. 80 Gary got a clean rag. He is just like a
hawk. We need the glue. Please put it in the back.

Introducing the Sound /f/

To make the sound /f/, place the top teeth firmly on the inside of the bottom lip; release the air continuously with no voice. (See Figure 25.)

Figure 25.
The sound /f/.

Listen to the examples and repeat them after the speaker.

EXAMPLES

fall	baffle	**ph**one	laug**h**
fish	puffed	tro**ph**y	laug**h**s
food	muff	Ral**ph**	laug**h**ed
fresh		Ral**ph**'s	toug**h**
flower	half		coug**h**
after		sap**ph**ire	
	often		

Practice for Mastery

Listen to the following sentences and repeat them after the speaker.

EXAMPLES

> Freddy found fresh flowers for his friend.
> Francie lifted her finger to show off her sapphire.
> Ralph's life is tough, but he laughs.
> Phil's life is soft, but he frets.
> He ate the fish and half a loaf of bread, then left.

Contrasting Sound Practice

Compare the sound /p/, from Unit Eighteen with /f/ by repeating the following words after the speaker.

EXAMPLES

/p/	/f/	/p/	/f/
pin	fin	pile	file
peel	feel	pour	four
pine	fine	pray	fray
paid	fade	pride	fried
pail	fail	pieced	feast
pare, pair, pear	fare, fair	pup	puff
peer	fear	sipped	sift
pork	fork	ripped	rift

Recognition Practice

The speaker will read four sentences on the tape. Circle the ones you hear, or repeat them now and do the written exercise later. The answers are on page 87.

1. Please peel this fruit.	Please feel this fruit.
2. It's a pine floor.	It's a fine floor.
3. She needs the pork to make the pie.	She needs the fork to make the pie.
4. How much is the pair?	How much is the fair?

Practice in Context

Now, after the speaker, repeat each line of the following poem featuring the /p/ and /f/ sounds.

> One fresh fall day
> Paul went to the fair
> To find some fun and food.
> But while hopping a fence
> He ripped his pants,
> Which put him in a foul mood.
> But he found a fine friend
> And prayed she would mend
> The rip before it could fray;
> And although he was pieced
> With a patch on the seat
> He went to the feast anyway.

Introducing the Sound /v/

To make the sound /v/, place the upper teeth against the inside of the lower lip, and release the air with a voiced sound. (See Figure 26.)

Figure 26.
The sound /v/.

Listen to the following examples, repeat them after the speaker, then listen for the confirmation.

EXAMPLES

vine	save	saves
vote	five	believes
favor	believe	saved
ever		loved
envy	of	

Usage Tip

• The contractions of <u>I have</u>, <u>you have</u>, <u>we have</u>, and <u>they have</u> are formed by adding an apostrophe ('ve) to the pronoun.

Listen to the examples and repeat them after the speaker.

EXAMPLES

I've been there.	(I have been there.)
You've seen it.	(You have seen it.)
We've won.	(We have won.)
They've gone.	(They have gone.)

Practice for Mastery

Listen to the following sentences and repeat them after the speaker.

EXAMPLES

Evelyn arrived in evening gloves at eleven.
Val survived the five-hour drive.
She is obviously envious, and I love it.
It takes a lot of nerve to drive over there in the van.
They've never voted in Virginia before.

Contrasting Sound Practice

Compare the sound /b/, from Unit Eighteen with /v/. Listen to the following words, and repeat them after the speaker.

EXAMPLES

/b/	/v/	/b/	/v/
bet	vet	ballet	valet
base	vase	bent	vent
berry, bury	very	best	vest
buys	vise	marble	marvel
bail, bale	veil, vale	Serbs	serves

Recognition Practice

Four sentences are recorded on the tape. Circle the ones you hear, or repeat them during the pauses and do the written exercise later. The answers are on page 87.

EXERCISE

1. She's a good bet.	She's a good vet.
2. We want to see the ballet.	We want to see the valet.
3. I only want the best.	I only want the vest.
4. Bev's bail was stiff.	Bev's veil was stiff.

Answers to Exercises

Recognition Practice, p. 84 Please feel this fruit. It's a pine floor. She needs the fork to make the pie. How much is the pair?
Recognition Practice, She's a good vet. We want to see the ballet. I only want the best. Bev's veil was stiff.

EXERCISE

1. She's a good bet.   She's a good vet.
2. We want to see   We want to see
   the ballet.   the valet.
3. I only want the best.   I only want the vest.
4. Bev's bail was stiff.   Bev's veil was stiff.

Answers to Exercises

Recognition Practice, p. 84 Please feel this fruit. It's a pine floor.
She needs the fork to make the pie. How much is the pair?
Recognition Practice, She's a good vet. We want to see the ballet.
I only want the best. Bev's veil was stiff.

Introducing the Sound /ch/

To make the sound /ch/, place the center of the tongue on the palate; stop the air completely, then release it abruptly with a voiceless sound. (See Figure 27.)

Figure 27.
The sound /ch/.

Listen to the examples and repeat them after the speaker.

EXAMPLES

chase	catch	question
chance	catching	
reaching	catches	
lunch	watched	
lunches		
reached		

When a word or syllable beginning with the sound /iuw/ follows the sound /t/, a /ch/ sound is formed.

Figure 28.
The sound /j/.

EXAMPLES

jam	germ	bridge	soldier
just	gym	judged	
ajar	agency	edges	
major	region		
	huge		

The sound /d/ followed by /iuw/ is pronounced /j/.

Listen to the examples and repeat them after the speaker.

EXAMPLES

education	did you	had you
graduate	would you	
individual	could you	

Practice for Mastery

Listen to the following sentences featuring the sound /j/ and then repeat them after the speaker.

EXAMPLES

I wanted you to come to my graduation.
Jim's *a* junior, majoring in education.
Would you please register at the gym?
Jill, in her jeans, jumped into her jeep.
Janice, did you see the soldier?

Introducing the Sound /sh/

To make the sound /sh/, touch the palate with the sides of the tongue and release the air slowly through the passageway formed down the center of the tongue. Do not stop the air flow. Do not make a sound with your voice. (See Figure 29.)

Figure 29.
The sound /sh/.

Listen to the following examples and repeat them after the speaker.

EXAMPLES

sugar	shame	mention	social
sure	shoe		special
	fashion	chef	
assure	wishes	chauffeur	ocean
issue	wished	machine	
anxious	tension		

Practice for Mastery

Listen to the following sentences featuring the sound /sh/, and repeat them after the speaker.

EXAMPLES

> Don't mention her anxious expression.
> Sean assured me he'd shine his shoes.
> Share the sugar with Charlotte.
> She wished she had gone shopping.

Practice in Context

Now say this poem, one line at a time, after the speaker.

Sharon and Charlotte shopped for shallots.
The shallots were shipped from chateaux.
Sharon shared the shallots
That were shipped in the box.
Should she share the champagne, too? No!

Contrasting Sound Practice

To compare /ch/ from Unit Twenty-two with /sh/, repeat the following words after the speaker.

EXAMPLES

/ch/	/sh/	/ch/	/sh/
chin	shin	cheek	chic
cheese	she's	which, witch	wish
choose	shoes	watch	wash
cheap	sheep	watches	washes
chair	share	matching	mashing
chop	shop	matched	mashed
chip	ship	crutch	crush

Recognition Practice

Four sentences are recorded on the tape. Below, circle the ones you hear, then check your work on page 95.

Exercise

1. Charles hurt his chin.   Charles hurt his shin.
2. This is your chair.   This is your share.
3. His witches are evil.   His wishes are evil.
4. Will you watch   Will you wash
   the baby?   the baby?

Introducing the Sound /zh/

To make the sound /**zh**/, touch your palate with the sides of your tongue and release the air slowly through the passageway formed down the center of the tongue. Do not stop the air. Make a sound with your voice. (See Figure 30.)

Figure 30.
The sound /zh/.

Listen to the following examples and repeat them after the speaker.

EXAMPLES

azure	measure	Asia	garage
	usual	vision	beige
		Persian	prestige
			regime
	equation	garages

This sound does not occur at the beginning of words.

Practice for Mastery

Listen to the following sentences featuring the sound /zh/, then repeat them after the speaker.

EXAMPLES

They usually watch television for pleasure.
She occasionally wears her beige blouse.
Take the usual measurements.
They found the treasure in Asia.

Answers to Exercise

Recognition Practice, p. 94 Charles hurt his shin. This is your chair. His wishes are evil. Will you watch the baby?

Introducing the Sound /s/

To make the sound /s/, place the center of your tongue against the palate and release the air slowly, but do not stop the air, and do not make a sound with your voice. (See Figure 31.)

Figure 31.
The sound /s/.

Listen to the following examples and repeat the words after the speaker.

EXAMPLES

say	**sc**ene	**c**ell
some		re**c**ent
square	kiss	a**c**id
small	missed	face
*e*ras*e*r	boss*e*s	
fast		walt**z**
leased	**p**sycho*l*ogy	walt**z**ed

The letter <u>x</u> is often pronounced as /k/ + /s/.

96

EXAMPLES

ax	e*x*pect	fix	fox	tuxedo
rela*x*ed	extr*a*			
sax*o*phone	exercise			

Be careful not to add a vowel sound before the /s/ at the beginning of a word. To avoid this, try pronouncing the /s/ at the end of the previous word.

Listen to the examples and repeat them after the speaker.

EXAMPLES

I s/peak S/pani*s*h. ("Ice peaks panish.")
Steve s/pends his pennies on s/tamps.
Scott s/kates at *a* s/pecial s/kating rink.
Stacy s/tays *i*n th*e* s/tates with her s/tepsist*e*r.

Usage Tips

- The final -s of plurals and third person (he, she, it) present tense verb forms is pronounced /s/ when it follows the voiceless consonant sounds /p/, /t/, /k/, /f/, and /θ/.
- The 's indicating possession or a contraction of <u>is</u> or <u>us</u> is also pronounced /s/ when it follows the voiceless consonants.

Listen to the following examples, repeat the words after the speaker, then listen for the confirmation.

Examples

Noun plurals	3rd-person singular verbs	Possessives and certain contractions
maps	tapes	Pat's
		Jack's
hats	hits	Ruth's
socks	cooks	
beliefs	looks	Miss Crist's
graphs	laughs	
baths		let's (let us)
wasps	grasps	it's (it is)
tests	tastes	that's (that is)
tasks	asks	what's (what is)

Practice for Mastery

Listen to the following sentences featuring the sound /s/, and repeat them after the speaker.

Examples

> Let's sew some snowsuits, said Sally.
> The sly fox sits in the forest and waits.
> Let's ask the guests for a list of requests.
> Miss Smith cooks the best feasts.
> Send Sue to the store on Saturday.
> Small Stephen still smiles sweetly.
> Stephanie slowly spins her sled in the snow.
> The Spanish speak Spanish in Spain.
> It's the worst snowstorm I've seen.

About the Letter s

The letter s is silent in the following words. Listen, and repeat each word after the speaker.

EXAMPLES

corps	chassis	chamois
aisle	debris	lisle

Contrasting Sound Practice

To compare the sound /sh/, from Unit Twenty-three, with /s/, repeat the following words.

EXAMPLES

/sh/	/s/	/sh/	/s/
shoot, chute	suit	she'll	seal
shed	said	shock	sock
shower	sour	ship	sip
shoe	sue	shine	sign
show	sew, sow, so	shelf	self
shame	same	shave	save
sheet	seat	leash	lease
she'd	seed	mesh	mess

Recognition Practice

Four sentences that feature these two sounds are recorded on the tape. Below, circle the ones you hear, then check your answers on page 106.

EXERCISE

1. It was a big shock.   It was a big sock.
2. Can you ship it?   Can you sip it?
3. Can you shave   Can you save
   my face?   my face?
4. They got good sheets. They got good seats.

Introducing the Sound /z/

To make the /z/ sound, place the center of the tongue against the palate; release the air slowly, without stopping. Make a sound with your voice.

Figure 32.
The sound /z/.

Listen to the following examples and repeat the words after the speaker.

EXAMPLES

zero	xerox	easy
lazy	xylophone	cousin
freeze	anxiety	cheese

Usage Tips

• Noun plurals, third person present tense verb forms, possessives, and contractions after vowels and the voiced consonants /b/, /d/, /g/, /v/, /m/, /n/, /ng/, /l/, /r/, and /d/ are spelled -s, and pronounced /z/.

Listen to the following examples and repeat them after the speaker.

EXAMPLES

Noun plurals	3rd-person singular verbs
potatoes	cries
labs	sees
heads	does
dogs	rides
leaves	leaves
rooms	breathes
cans	comes
things	runs
prisms	

Possessives	Contractions with <u>is</u>
Bob's	he's
Peg's	she's
Martha's	
his	
hers	
yours	
ours	
theirs	

Listen to the following sentences featuring the sound /z/, and repeat them after the speaker.

EXAMPLES

She's my friend's cousin.
He reads newspapers and magazines on Thursdays.
He loves his new toys.
Susan's cousin leaves on Wednesday.

• The letter <u>x</u> is sometimes pronounced as /g/ + /z/

EXAMPLES

examine	exaggerate	exert
exact	exist	

• The sounds /s/ and /z/ can indicate the difference between a noun and a verb. Repeat the following examples after the speaker.

EXAMPLES

Nouns—/s/	**Verbs—/z/**
abuse	abuse
advice	advise
excuse	excuse
grease	grease
house	house
use	use

Practice for Mastery

Now repeat these sentences after the speaker.

EXAMPLES

We can house five of your guests at our beach house.
There is no use for that gadget. I can't use it.
Victims of abuse sometimes learn to abuse others.
When I asked him for advice, he advised me to keep quiet.
We excused him that time, but there was no excuse for his behavior.

Contrasting Sound Practice

Compare the sound /s/ with the sound /z/ by repeating the following words after the speaker.

EXAMPLES

/s/	/z/	/s/	/z/
sip	zip	place	plays
Sue	zoo	cease	sees
loose	lose	raced	raised
rice	rise		

Usage Tip

• After the sounds /s/, /sh/, /z/, /zh/, /ch/ and /j/, add the unstressed vowel /ə/ before the grammatical -s. The combined sound /əz/ adds one syllable to the word.

Listen to the following examples, repeat them after the speaker, then listen for the confirmation.

EXAMPLES

Noun plurals	3rd-person singular verbs	Possessives
glasses	kisses	Bruce's
wishes	brushes	Trish's
bruises	praises	Rose's
garages	massages	Solange's
churches	matches	Mrs. Gooch's
pages	stages	Page's

Practice for Mastery

Listen to the following sentences featuring the sound /əz/ and repeat them after the speaker.

EXAMPLES

He washes his cars in Charles's garages.
She teaches Bruce's niece's friend.
Rose's daughter wishes she had new glasses.
Mrs. Jones faxes pages of messages to our offices.
All of Mrs. Watkins's watches are Rolexes.

Practice in Context

Listen to the following poems which feature the sounds /s/, /z/, and /əz/, and repeat them line by line during the pauses.

The Supermarket (Plural Nouns)

What's in the store?
/s/
Carrots, beets,
Grapes, meats,
Drinks, cakes,
Soups, sweets,
Leeks, soaps,
Lots of treats.
/z/
Onions, potatoes,
Cans of tomatoes,
Breads, medicines,
Vegetables, like peas,
Non-food items,
All kinds of cheese.
/əz/
Lettuces, radishes,
Packages, juices,
Peaches, matches,
Good things for all uses.
Spices, low prices,
Some surprises,
No abuses.

The Doll (Third-person Singular Verbs)

What does she do?
/s/
She laughs, talks,
Wets, walks,
Sleeps, drinks,
Eats, blinks,
And asks for nothing.
/z/
She soothes, cries,
Lies in the crib,
Smiles, sings,
Comfort brings.
/əz/
She dances, entrances,
Amuses, amazes,
And causes no trouble.

The Lost and Found
(Possessives and Contractions)

/s/
Whose coat is this?
It's Jack's or Rick's.
And that one?
That's either Pat's or Mick's.
This hat's pretty,
Is it Miss Smith's?
It looks like the kind
She always picks.
/z/
These shoes are big
They might be John's.
But they could be
His brother Tom's.
Who knows whose things
Are in these rooms?
Those sweaters are probably

Old Ms. Blume's.
/əz/
Galoshes, britches,
sashes, watches,
Are they Rose's,
Or Mrs. Dodge's?
They could be Charles's
Or Mrs. Welsh's,
But they're more likely
Someone else's.

Answers to Exercise

Recognition Practice, p. 99 It was a big shock. Can you sip it? Can you save my face? They got good seats.

Introducing the Sound /l/

To pronounce /l/, curl your tongue up; put the under side of the tongue firmly on the back of your top teeth and make a sound with your voice. (See Figure 33.)

Figure 33.
The sound /l/.

Listen to the examples and repeat them after the speaker.

EXAMPLES

lake	daily	clean	male	yellow
love	solve	glass	animal	filled
	shelf	place	alcohol	will
	film			

Usage Tip

- The subject pronouns plus -'ll form contractions with the final /l/ sound of <u>will</u>, indicating some instances of future time.

Listen to the examples and repeat them after the speaker.

EXAMPLES

I'll	she'll	we'll
you'll	it'll	they'll
he'll		

Practice for Mastery

Listen to the following sentences featuring the sound /l/, and repeat them after the speaker.

EXAMPLES

Lou delayed the long flight.
Lola likes to laugh a lot.
That fellow, Luke, loves the bowling alley.
She'll like the lovely landscape.
We'll help you fill the glasses.

About the Letter l

The letter l is silent in the following words. Listen, and repeat each word after the speaker.

EXAMPLES

half	could	Lincoln
halves	should	
salve	would	

Introducing the Sound /r/

To make the sound /r/, keep the tongue back; do not let your tongue touch inside your mouth; round your lips and push them forward. Make a voiced sound. (See Figure 34.)

Figure 34.
The sound /r/.

Listen to the examples and repeat them after the speaker.

EXAMPLES

race	cry	around
ride	draw	carol
	from	
write	green	mirror
	price	
	try	colonel
	through	
bird	pair	fears
orphan	more	fires
surprise	martyr	
		cared
		fired

Usage Tips

• The grammar markers -s and -ed are voiced after /r/.

Listen to the following examples and repeat them after the speaker.

EXAMPLES

/r/ + /z/	/r/ + /d/
fears	feared
cares	cared
fires	fired
implores	implored
lures	lured

• /r/ plus <u>e</u> is a prefix that indicates "to do again."

Listen to the examples and repeat them after the speaker.

EXAMPLES

re-do	re-decorate
re-peat	re-write

• <u>e</u> or <u>o</u> (both pronounced /ə/) plus /r/ is a noun marker meaning "a person who does something."

Listen to the examples and repeat them after the speaker.

EXAMPLES

teacher	sinner	actor	executor
preacher	reader	doctor	
lawyer	speeder	tutor	

• <u>e</u> plus /r/ at the end of an adjective indicates its comparative form.

Listen to the examples and repeat them after the speaker.

EXAMPLES

taller	older	shorter	younger
richer	faster	poorer	slower
sweeter	happier	dearer	sillier
nicer	friendlier	newer	cozier

• -r at the end of a pronoun can indicate possession.

Listen to the examples and repeat them after the speaker.

EXAMPLES

your	her
our	their

• 're indicates a contraction of the verb <u>are</u>.

Listen to the examples and repeat them after the speaker.

EXAMPLES

you're	they're
we're	there're

Practice for Mastery

Listen to the following sentences featuring the sound /r/ and repeat them after the speaker.

EXAMPLES

Rita read three very short stories.
Roger, the writer, brought thirty red roses.
Remember to write to your friends.
Robert ran to the store for his mother.
There're prettier flowers at the florist's.
We're here to remember our father.

Contrasting Sound Practice

To compare the sound /l/ with the sound /r/, repeat the following words after the speaker.

EXAMPLES

/l/	/r/
led, lead	red, read
lift	rift
liver	river
laughed	raft
light	right, write
low	row
alive	arrive
believe	bereave
belly	berry
plays	prays, praise
climb	crime
clam	cram
flight	fright
label	labor
pale, pail	pare, pair, pear

Recognition Practice

Ten words featuring /l/ and /r/ sounds are recorded next on the tape. Below, circle the words you hear, then check your answers on page 113.

EXERCISE

1. alive	arrive	6. flight	fright
2. led	red	7. plays	prays
3. climb	crime	8. pail	pair
4. laughed	raft	9. liver	river
5. light	right	10. belly	berry

Dictation Practice

You will hear six sentences on the tape. During the pauses, write them on a piece of paper, then check them below.

Practice in Context

Now repeat this poem, one line at a time, to practice /l/ and /r/.

What'll you have?

I'll have lemon pie, with lots of meringue on the top.

You'll get fat; you'll get sick; you'll be sorry tomorrow.

Never mind. I'll have diet pop.

Answers to Exercises

Recognition Practice, p. 112 arrive; red; climb; laughed; right; flight; plays; pair, pare, or pear; river; belly

Dictation Practice, Laura plays all day. It was a low house. Please get me a pear. Is it right yet? Can you lead them? The teacher collected the tests.

Introducing the Sound /m/

To produce the sound /m/, press your lips together and make a voiced, humming sound; release the air through your nose. (See Figure 35.)

Figure 35.
The sound /m/.

Listen to the following examples and repeat them after the speaker.

EXAMPLES

maybe	tomorrow	name	games	comb
mother	famous	them	tamed	climb
		him	camp	
		from		

Usage Tip

- I'm = I am. The sound /m/ is the contracted verb in the sentence.

Practice for Mastery

Listen to the following sentences featuring the sound /m/, and repeat them after the speaker.

EXAMPLES

> My name is Emily.
> Maybe my mother will make something.
> I'm coming home with them tomorrow.
> My roommate is from Maine.
> I'm from Alabama.

Introducing the Sound /n/

To pronounce /n/, place your tongue against your palate and hold it there; make a voiced sound and release the air through your nose. (See Figure 36.)

Figure 36.
The sound /n/.

Listen to the examples and repeat them after the speaker.

EXAMPLES

name	any	and	sane	plains
never	money	angel	then	trained
		interest	envy	
know	funny	thin		

Usage Tips

• **-n** is added to the indefinite article <u>a</u> before words that begin with vowels.

Listen to the examples and repeat them after the speaker.

EXAMPLES

*a*n apple	*a*n orange	*a*n extra book

• **n**'t is added to the verb <u>to be</u> and to auxiliary verbs to make negative contractions.

EXAMPLES

aren't	wouldn't	isn't
weren't	shouldn't	hasn't
don't	couldn't	wasn't
can't	didn't	doesn't
	hadn't	mustn't
	mightn't	

• **-en** is the past participle marker for many verbs.

Listen to the examples and repeat them after the speaker.

EXAMPLES

taken	given	frozen
eaten	gotten	proven
driven		

Practice for Mastery

Listen to the following sentences featuring the sound /n/, and repeat them after the speaker.

EXAMPLES

> The sun shines.
> The thin man is an African dancer.
> Mine is fine.
> Tony has taken the train.
> Nancy has many new friends.
> They haven't eaten the tuna

About the Letter n

The letter n is silent in the following words. Listen, and repeat each word after the speaker.

EXAMPLES

autumn	column	hymn

Contrasting Sound Practice

To compare /m/ with /n/, repeat the following words after the speaker.

EXAMPLES

/m/	/n/	/m/	/n/
might	night	hem	hen
mere	near	lame	lane
dime	dine	simmer	sinner

Recognition Practice

Four sentences featuring the sounds /m/ and /n/ are recorded next on the tape. Circle the ones you hear, then check your answers on page 122.

EXERCISE

1. I'm doing the same | I'm doing the sane
thing. | thing

2. We would love a | We would love a
little sum. | little son.

3. She brought a hem | She brought a hen
for me to fix. | for me to fix.

4. The dimmer's on | The dinner's on
the table. | the table.

Introducing the Sound /ŋ/

To make the sound /ŋ/, bring the back of
your tongue up against the velum, close the air off
completely, and release it through the nose. (See
Figure 37.)

Figure 37.
The sound /ŋ/.

Listen to the examples and repeat them after the
speaker.

EXAMPLES

long	hanger	tongue
strong	singer	
singing	belonged	
going	belongings	

A double consonant sound is formed when /ng/ is followed by the sounds /g/ or /k/.

Listen to the examples and repeat them after the speaker.

EXAMPLES

finger	stronger	thanking	sinking
longer	tangle	thinking	drinking

There are three consonant sounds together in the following words. Listen, and repeat them after the speaker.

EXAMPLES

thanked	anxious
(ŋ + k + t)	(ŋ + k + sh)

Usage Tip

• -ing is added to the verb to form the present participle.

Listen to the examples and repeat them after the speaker.

EXAMPLES

I'm going.
She's looking.
They were shopping.

We have been looking.
The book is interesting.
The movie was fascinating.

Practice for Mastery

Listen to the following sentences featuring the sound /ŋ/ and repeat them after the speaker.

EXAMPLES

The singer sang too many long songs.
Your fingers are longer and stronger than mine
The rings belong on the singer's finger.

Contrasting Sound Practice

Now compare the sound /m/ with the sound /ŋ/ by repeating the following words.

EXAMPLES

/m/	/ŋ/	/m/	/ŋ/
rim	ring	swimmer	swinger
rum	rung	simmer	singer
sum, some	sung	Sam	sang
swim	swing		

Recognition Practice

Listen to the four sentences recorded on the tape and, below, circle the ones you hear. The answers are on page 122.

EXERCISE

1. He gave me a rim   He gave me a ring
   last week.   last week.

2. She's dating a swimmer.	She's dating a swinger.
3. She said she could swim it.	She said she could swing it.
4. Mama has some good songs.	Mama has sung good songs

Contrasting Sound Practice

Compare /n/ and /ŋ/ by repeating the following words after the speaker.

EXAMPLES

/n/	/ŋ/	/n/	/ŋ/
lawn	long	stun	stung
run	rung	thin	thing
fan	fang	sin	sing

Recognition Practice

Below, circle the four sentences you hear on the tape, then check your work on page 122.

EXERCISE

1. It was a lawn party.	It was a long party.
2. It hurts him to sin.	It hurts him to sing.
3. I think she has fans.	I think she has fangs.
4. He has run four times.	He has rung four times.

Contrasting Sound Practice

Compare /m/, /n/, and /ŋ/ by repeating the following words after the speaker.

EXAMPLES

/m/	/n/	/ŋ/
rum	run	rung
Sam	San	sang
simmer	sinner	singer
some	son, sun	sung
whim	win	wing

Practice in Context

Listen to the following dialogue featuring the sounds /m/, /n/, and /ŋ/, and repeat each line after the speakers.

—Sam, how is your son?
—He's fine, thanks! You know, he's nineteen now.
—What's he doing?
—He's going to the University of New Mexico and he's planning to be an engineer.
—When is he coming home?
—He's coming soon, on the ninth of June.

Answers to Exercises

Recognition Practice, p. 118 I'm doing the sane thing. We would love a little sum. She brought a hem for me to fix. The dimmer's on the table.
Recognition Practice, p. 120 He gave me a rim last week. She's dating a swimmer. She said she could swing it. Mama has sung good songs.
Recognition Practice, p. 121 It was a lawn party. It hurts him to sing. I think she has fans. He has rung four times.

Introducing the Sound /θ/

To make the sound /θ/, hold the tip of your tongue between your top and bottom teeth; force the air out with a voiceless sound. (See Figure 38.)

Figure 38.
The sound /θ/.

Listen to the following examples and repeat them after the speaker.

EXAMPLES

thank	tru**th**ful	heal**th**	bir**th**s
thing	weal**th**y	tee**th**	dea**th**s
thirsty	no**th**ing	mon**th**	
	some**th**ing		

Usage Tips

- -**th**, pronounced /θ/, can indicate the noun form of an adjective.

Listen to the next examples and repeat them after the speaker.

123

EXAMPLES

width	(wide)	strength	(strong)
depth	(deep)	breadth	(broad)
length	(long)		

- -th , pronounced /θ/, indicates all the ordinal numbers except for <u>first</u>, <u>second</u>, and <u>third</u>, and combinations that end with <u>first</u>, <u>second</u>, and <u>third</u>. It also indicates all fractions except for <u>half</u> and <u>third</u>.

Listen to the following examples and repeat them after the speaker.

EXAMPLES

fourth	fifteenth	eightieth
fifth	sixteenth	ninetieth
sixth	seventeenth	hundredth
seventh	eighteenth	thousandth
eighth	nineteenth	millionth
ninth	twentieth	
tenth	thirtieth	one-fourth
eleventh	fortieth	three-fifths
twelfth	fiftieth	seven-eighths
thirteenth	sixtieth	
fourteenth	seventieth	

Practice for Mastery

Listen to the following sentences featuring the sound /θ/ and repeat them after the speaker.

EXAMPLES

We both need something for our throats.
He thought thirty thousand dollars was nothing.
She took an oath to tell the truth.

Thanksgiving is on the fourth Thursday of the
month of November.
Mathematics is one of her strengths.
He may be wealthy, but he's ruthless and uncouth.

Contrasting Sound Practice

Compare the sound /s/, from Unit Twenty-four,
with the sound /θ/ by repeating the following words
after the speaker.

EXAMPLES

/s/	/θ/	/s/	/θ/
sin	thin	miss	myth
sing	thing	mass	math
sink	think	pass	path
sought	thought	mouse	mouth
sank	thank	force	forth, fourth
sum	thumb	truce	truth
seem, seam	theme		

Recognition Practice

Four sentences featuring the sounds /s/ and /θ/
are recorded next on the tape. Below, circle the ones
you hear, then check your answers on page 128.

EXERCISE

1. The truce is
   important.
2. I sought it out.
3. He can't find
   the pass.
4. Show the teacher
   your seam.

The truth is
important.
I thought it out.
He can't find
the path.
Show the teacher
your theme.

Introducing the Sound /ð/

To pronounce /ð/, hold the tip of your tongue between your top and bottom teeth; release the air with a voiced sound. (See Figure 39.)

Figure 39.
The sound /ð/.

Listen to the following examples and repeat them after the speaker.

EXAMPLES

they	lather	bathe	bathes
these	together	clothe	clothes
those	breathing	breathe	soothed
the	rhythm		

Practice for Mastery

Listen to the following sentences featuring the consonant /ð/, and repeat them after the speaker.

EXAMPLES

The mother soothed the teething baby.
My brother loathes this weather.
Father seethed when he saw these leather pants.

About the Letters th

The letters th are silent in the following words. Listen, and repeat each word after the speaker.

EXAMPLES

asthma	isthmus

Contrasting Sound Practice

Now compare the sound /d/, from Unit Nineteen, with the sound /ð/. Repeat the words after the speaker.

EXAMPLES

/d/	/ð/
dare	there, their, they're
dough	though
den	then
ladder	lather
wetter	weather, whether
letter	leather
utter, udder	other
fodder	father
mutter	mother
writing, riding	writhing
breed	breathe
sued	soothe
seed	seethe
skating	scathing

Recognition Practice

Listen carefully to the following four sentences on the tape, and circle below the ones you hear. Check your work on page 128.

EXERCISE

---

1. Did you see the letter? | Did you see the leather?
2. He made a big ladder. | He made a big lather.
3. Yes, they sued him. | Yes, they soothe him.
4. It was his mutter that bothered her. | It was his mother that bothered her.

Answers to Exercises

Recognition Practice, p. 125 The truce is important. I sought it out. He can't find the path. Show the teacher your seam.

Recognition Practice, Did you see the letter? He made a big ladder. Yes, they soothe him. It was his mutter that bothered her.

Introducing the Sound /h/

To make the sound /h/, keep your tongue free and force air from the throat with a voiced sound. (See Figure 40.)

Figure 40.
The sound /h/.

Listen to the examples and repeat them after the speaker.

EXAMPLES

hay	mahogany	who
hill	Ohio	whole
hope	alcohol	
huge	preheat	
hurry		

When the words <u>he</u>, <u>her</u>, <u>his</u>, <u>him</u>, and <u>has</u> are unstressed, the /h/ sound is often not pronounced.

Listen to the examples, and repeat them after the speaker.

EXAMPLES

> I don't know where (h)e is.
> He gave it to (h)er yesterday.
> I haven't seen (h)im.

Practice for Mastery

Listen to the following sentences and repeat them after the speaker.

EXAMPLES

> Does (h)e have any hope?
> Hi! What's *your* hurry?
> Howard is hiding in Ohio.
> They have *a* huge hotel *at* Lake Tahoe.
> Her husband brought home *a* huge mahogany hutch.

About the Letter h

The letter h is silent in the following examples. Listen, and repeat each word after the speaker.

EXAMPLES

honor, honest	vehement
herb	exhaust
heir	exhort
hour	exhume
	shepherd
John	what
oh, ah	when
night, fight, etc.	where
though, through, etc.	why
caught, bought, etc.	khaki
	rhythm
	thyme

Introducing the Sound /w/

To make the sound /w/, relax your tongue, then round your lips and press them back against the front of your teeth. Make a sound as you release your lips. (See Figure 41.)

Figure 41.
The sound /w/.

Listen to the examples and repeat them after the speaker.

EXAMPLES

way	*a*way	queen
was		
		sweet
		twenty
where	*a*while	one
why		once
whistl*e*		

Practice for Mastery

Listen to the following sentences featuring the sound /w/, and repeat them after the speaker.

EXAMPLES

> **W**hen will we go *a*way?
> The wind whistled in the woods.
> Dwight and Duane went to Guam.
> Why was there a war?
> One of the twins walked twenty miles.
> Wanda wore her white dress on Wednesday.
> I went for a walk with Walter McGuire.

About the Letter w

The letter w is silent in the following words. Listen, and repeat each word after the speaker.

EXAMPLES

who, whom, whose, whole	two
wren, write, wrong	toward
sword	knowledge

Practice in Context

Repeat this poem after the speaker, one line at a time, to practice /w/.

> Why do we have an h in *why*,
>   and *where*, *when*, *what*, and *white*?
> Well, there's a w in *who*, *whose*, and *whole*,
>   and *write* when the meaning is right.

Contrasting Sound Practice

Compare the sound /v/, from Unit Twenty-one, with the sound /w/, by repeating the following words after the speaker.

EXAMPLES

/v/	/w/	/v/	/w/
vine	wine	vow	wow
very, vary	wary	vile	while
veal	wheel, we'll	veer	we're
vent	went	vest	west
vase	ways, weighs		

Recognition Practice

Four sentences featuring the previous sounds /v/ and /w/ are recorded next on the tape. Below, circle the ones you hear, then check your answers on page 136.

EXERCISE

1. He took the veal.   He took the wheel.
2. It's in the vest.   It's in the west.
3. What's the vine like?   What's the wine like?
4. Veer to the left.   We're to the left.

Introducing the Sound /y/

To pronounce /y/, spread your tongue flat and toward the back of your mouth; do not let your tongue touch the palate. Next, make a wide smile with your lips and bring your tongue forward with a voiced sound. (See Figure 42.)

Figure 42.
The sound /y/.

Listen to the following examples and repeat them after the speaker.

EXAMPLES

yes	yet	mayor
yellow	year	beyond

When the sound /y/ is followed by the vowel sound /u/, the combination is exactly the same as the vowel sound /iuw/.

Listen to the examples and repeat them after the speaker.

EXAMPLES

you	youth	use	Utah

Practice for Mastery

Listen to the following sentences featuring the sound /y/, and repeat them after the speakers.

EXAMPLES

May I use **your** iron?
Yes, you may use it any time.
He's **a** popular hockey play**er** at th**e** university
this **year**.
Th**e** Miami law**yer** w**as** triumph**a**nt **yesterday**.

About the Letter y

The letter y is silent in the following words. Listen,
and repeat each word after the speaker.

EXAMPLES

says	prayers

Contrasting Sound Practice

Compare the sound /j/ from Unit Twenty-two,
with the sound /y/ by repeating the following words.

EXAMPLES

/j/	/y/	/j/	/y/
jeer	year	joke	yoke
jello	yellow	jet	yet
major	mayor	gel	yell
jam	yam	jot	yacht

Recognition Practice

Four sentences using the sounds /j/ and /y/ are
recorded next on the tape. Circle the ones you hear
and check your answers on page 136.

EXERCISE

1. There's no juice.	There's no use.
2. My uncle is the major.	My uncle is the mayor.
3. Has he come by jet?	Has he come by yet?
4. Are you going to jail?	Are you going to Yale?

Practice in Context

Now, repeat the following poem after the speaker, one line at a time, to practice /j/ and /y/.

> Jeremy bought a yellow jet,
> And then he got a yacht.
> "Why did you get the yacht," asked Brett,
> "When you haven't used the yellow jet yet?"

Answers to Exercises

Recognition Practice, p. 133 He took the wheel. It's in the vest. What's the wine like? We're to the left.
Recognition Practice, There's no use. My uncle is the major. Has he come by yet? Are you going to jail?

Sometimes a word ending in a consonant sound is followed by a word beginning with the same consonant sound, or one formed in the same position. To pronounce these "double consonants," do not release the sound between words. Emphasize the sound by holding it a little longer.

Listen to the following examples, and repeat them after the speaker.

Examples

/p/ + /p/	Keep practicing
/b/ + /b/	Grab Brian's hand.
/p/ + /b/	That pup belongs to her.
/t/ + /t/	It's not too much.
/d/ + /d/	Dad didn't tell me.
/t/ + /d/	Don't do that.
/k/ + /k/	I like candy.
/g/ + /g/	That rug goes here.
/k/ + /g/	They like green apples.
/f/ + /f/	Keep off Freddie's flowers.
/v/ + /v/	I love Vermont.
/v/ + /f/	He has lots of friends.
/s/ + /s/	That's scary.
/z/ + /z/	His zeroes are in the wrong place.
/z/ + /s/	His science class is interesting.
/l/ + /l/	He'll like it.
/r/ + /r/	They are wrong.
/m/ + /m/	We named him Mike.
/n/ + /n/	Dan knows the truth.
/θ/ + /θ/	Are you going with three bags?
/θ/ + /ð/	He left with the dog.

There are two exceptions to this pattern. The sounds /ch/ and /j/ must be released before pronouncing another word.

Listen to the examples and repeat them after the speaker.

EXAMPLES

/ch/ + /ch/	I can't reach Charles.
/j/ + /j/	Will you judge Jack's team?
/ch/ + /j/	She's going to teach geometry.

PART THREE
STRESS PATTERNS

English words can be divided into syllables. Each spoken vowel sound makes one syllable. A syllable can be

- a vowel sound alone,
- a vowel before a consonant,
- a vowel after a consonant, or
- a vowel between consonants.

Listen to these examples of one-syllable words and repeat them after the speaker.

EXAMPLES

Vowel alone	oh	I	
Vowel-consonant	on	ice	
Consonant-vowel	to	be	you
Consonant-vowel-Consonant	big	tough	cute

Each syllable in a word has a degree of emphasis, called stress. There are three stress levels, primary (/), secondary (/), and unstressed (–).

Each word of two or more syllables has one syllable that is longer and louder than the others. It has primary stress. In the examples that follow, these syllables are represented in **extra bold letters**.

Some words and syllables have secondary stress, which is slightly weaker than the primary one, but louder and longer than an unstressed one. These syllables are represented in **bold letters** in the examples.

There are many unstressed syllables in English. They have a short, soft vowel sound and may be difficult to hear at first. They are represented in the examples in Roman type. Unstressed vowels pronounced /ə/ are in *italics*. Be careful to emphasize any consonants that occur with unstressed vowels.

Introducing Primary Stress

A word with two vowel sounds has two syllable
One syllable has primary stress. Say it a little loude
and longer than the other. Pronounce the vowel wit
importance.

The vowel of the unstressed syllable is usually pro
nounced /ə/, no matter how it is spelled. Make th
vowel sound short. Pronounce the consonant soun
clearly and distinctly.

Listen to the following examples and repeat the
after the speaker.

EXAMPLES

Primary stress on first syllable		Primary stress on second syllable	
/	**–**	**–**	**/**
cli-	m*a*te	*ad*-	**vice**
ac-	t*o*r	*ex*-	**cite**
pleas-	*u*re	*con*-	**fused**
sol-	d*i*er	*sup*-	**pose**
danc-	*e*s	*sur*-	**prised**
wash-	*e*s		
watch-	*e*s		
fold-	*e*d		
seat-	*e*d		

The sounds /iy/, /ow/, /iuw/, and /ɪ/ often kee
their normal pronunciations in unstressed syllables.

Listen to the following examples and repeat the
after the speaker.

EXAMPLES

Stress on first syllable		Stress on second syllable	
/	**–**	**–**	**/**
/iy/			
ar-	my	re-	**peat**
ba-	by	de-	**duct**
ci-	ty	be-	**gin**
/ow/			
ar-	row	o-	**bey**
el-	bow	o-	**mit**
fol-	low	o-	**kay**
/iuw/			
ar-	gue	u-	**nique**
neph-	ew		
val-	ue		
/ı/			
build-	ing	in-	**stead**
den-	tist	in-	**sist**
mu-	sic	im-	**mune**

Usage Tip

• The stress patterns **/ –** and **– /** indicate the difference between certain nouns and verbs.

Listen to the following examples and repeat them after the speaker.

EXAMPLES

Nouns		Verbs	
/	**–**	**–**	**/**
pres-	*e*nt	pre-	**sent**
reb-	*e*l	re-	**bel**
ob-	ject	ob-	**ject**
prog-	ress	pro-	**gress**
rec-	*o*rd	re-	**cord**

To practice the difference in stress between nouns and verbs, repeat the following sentences after the speaker.

EXAMPLES

> We're going to present him with a present at the reception.
> His brother is a rebel. He rebels against all the established rules.
> If you don't object, I will put several objects on the table.
> "When did you record your last record?," the boy asked the singer.

Introducing Secondary Stress

Some two-syllable words have **primary** stress on the first syllable and **secondary** stress on the second syllable. Say the first syllable strongly. Emphasize the second syllable a little less, but say it with a clear vowel.

Listen to the examples and repeat them after the speaker.

EXAMPLES

❘	ˌ
ac-	cent
ath-	lete
fe-	male
in-	come
in-	sect
trans-	fer

Usage Tips

- The stress pattern ❘ ˌ is common for compound words, whether they are spelled with or without a hyphen.

Listen to the examples and repeat them after the speaker.

EXAMPLES

Nouns		Verbs		Adjectives	
/	/	/	/	/	/
air-	plane	dry-	clean	bare-	foot
bird-	house	black-	mail	care-	free
black-	board	brain-	wash	fore-	most
drug-	store	down-	grade	home-	sick
hot-	dog	foot-	note	new-	born
land-	lord	kid-	nap		
make-	up				
rail-	road				

• The stress patterns **/ /** and **– /** indicate the differences between some nouns and verbs.

Listen to the examples and repeat them after the speaker.

EXAMPLES

Nouns		Verbs	
/	/	–	/
com-	bine	com-	**bine**
com-	pact	com-	**pact**
con-	duct	con-	**duct**
con-	flict	con-	**flict**
con-	tract	con-	**tract**
con-	trast	con-	**trast**
con-	vert	con-	**vert**
dis-	count	dis-	**count**
per-	mit	per-	**mit**
pro-	test	pro-	**test**
sus-	pect	sus-	**pect**

Now repeat these sentences to practice the noun-verb differences in stress.

EXAMPLES

> The student's conduct was unacceptable.
> The teacher had to conduct him to the principal.
> We signed a contract to buy the house.
> Now we have to contract an architect to
> remodel it.
> The young boy's father wouldn't permit him to
> get a driver's permit.
> I suspect he is one of the suspects.

• The stress patterns **/ /** and **/ –** are important for distinguishing the "teen" numbers from the "tens." Note also that they have different pronunciations of the letter t.

Listen to the next examples and repeat them after the speaker.

EXAMPLES

Teens		Tens	
/	**/**	**/**	**–**
thir-	teen	thir-	ty
four-	teen	for-	ty
fif-	teen	fif-	ty
six-	teen	six-	ty
eigh-	teen	eigh-	ty
nine-	teen	nine-	ty

(seventeen and seventy have an additional unstressed syllable.)

Say the following poem, one line at a time, after the speaker, to practice the tens and teens.

EXAMPLES

Have you seen my teen?
She's a high school queen
Between sixteen and seventeen.
She can be flirty, act like thirty,
Or a baby, then a lady,
She makes her mother feel like eighty,
Or eighteen.

• The stress patterns / / and **/** / distinguish compound words from other modified nouns.

Listen to the examples that follow and repeat them after the speaker.

EXAMPLES

Compound word	Modifier + noun
/ /	/ **/**
greenhouse	green house
bluebird	blue bird
darkroom	dark room
hotdog	hot dog
blackboard	black board

Listen to these sentences, which compare compound nouns with other modified nouns, and repeat them after the speaker.

EXAMPLES

The kitchen was a dark room.
There was a darkroom in the basement for
photos.
I saw a blue bird in the yard.
I don't think it was a bluebird.
They bought a new house with a greenhouse
and a birdbath in the back.

I live in a white house, but it's not The White
House.
He said a few cross words when he couldn't
finish the crossword puzzle.
It was 100°, and Rover was one hot dog.
Hotdogs are great at baseball games.

- Some words have secondary stress on the first
  syllable, and primary on the second.

Listen to the examples and repeat them after the
speaker.

EXAMPLES

/	/	/	/
car-	**toon**	un-	**do**
cash-	**ier**	un-	**pack**
Chin-	**ese**	up-	**date**
post-	**pone**	with-	**draw**

- Verbs with the prefix <u>re</u>, when it means "to do
  again," also have / **/** as a stress pattern.

Listen to the examples and repeat them after the
speaker.

EXAMPLES

/	/	/	/	/	/
re-	**build**	re-	**play**	re-	**wind**
re-	**do**	re-	**set**	re-	**word**
re-	**check**	re-	**tell**	re-	**write**
re-	**heat**	re-	**think**		

- Some verbs followed by prepositions have special
  meanings, and are called <u>two-word</u> verbs. They
  too have the / **/** stress pattern.

Listen to the examples and repeat them after the
speaker.

EXAMPLES

/	/	/	/	/	/
back	up	find	out	put	off
back	down	give	back	slow	down
back	off	give	in	take	in
call	off	give	up	take	out
calm	down	hand	in	take	off
clean	up	hand	out	use	up
dream	up	leave	out	wind	up
dress	up	put	on		

Practice for Mastery

Now repeat the following sentences featuring the
/ / stress pattern.

EXAMPLES

After we unpack, we'll play Chinese checkers.

I'm going to the cashier to withdraw the money.

She will rewind the cartoon for you.

We'll retest your blood and postpone your
routine exam.

Please slow down, or we'll wind up on the side
of the road.

Let's find out if we can take off next week.

I'll call off the next party if you don't clean up
after this one.

Words with three or more syllables have one syllable with primary stress. The other syllables are either all unstressed, or one has secondary stress and the rest are unstressed.

Introducing Stress Pattern 1

Primary stress is on the first syllable and all other syllables are unstressed.

Listen to these examples of three-syllable words and repeat them after the speaker.

EXAMPLES

/	–	–		/	–	–
a-	ni-	mal		**fin-**	ish-	es
cho-	co-	late		**vis-**	i-	ted
fur-	ni-	ture		**vis-**	i-	tor
hos-	pi-	tal		**dir-**	ti-	er
vege-	ta-	ble		**bus-**	i-	est
vis-	it-	ing		**care-**	ful-	ly
or-	ang	-es				

Listen to the following examples of four-syllable words with pattern 1, and repeat them after the speaker.

EXAMPLES

/	–	–	–		/	–	–	–
for-	tu-	nate-	ly		**per-**	man-	ent-	ly
in-	no-	cent-	ly		**ser-**	i-	ous-	ly

Introducing Stress Pattern 2

Primary stress is on the second syllable and all other syllables are unstressed.

Listen to the following examples of three-syllable words and repeat them after the speaker.

EXAMPLES

–	/	–		–	/	–
a-	**part-**	ment		ex-	**am-**	ple
ba-	**na-**	na		pro-	**hi-**	bit
con-	**di-**	tion		to-	**ge-**	ther
de-	**ci-**	sion				

Next, listen to examples of four-syllable words with pattern 2, and repeat them after the speaker.

EXAMPLES

–	/	–	–		–	/	–	–
com-	**mu-**	ni-	ty		o-	**ri-**	gin-	al
e-	**mer-**	gen-	cy		me-	**chan-**	i-	cal
ex-	**per-**	i-	ence		se-	**cu-**	ri-	ty
in-	**fer-**	i-	or					

Following are some five-syllable words with pattern 2. Repeat them after the speaker.

EXAMPLES

–	/	–	–	–
af-	**fec-**	tion-	ate-	ly
con-	**si-**	der-	a-	ble
con-	**di-**	tion-	al-	ly
co-	**op-**	er-	a-	tive
in-	**ev-**	it-	a-	ble
pro-	**fes-**	sion-	al-	ly

Introducing Stress Pattern 3

Primary stress is on the first syllable and secondary stress is on the third syllable. All other syllables are unstressed.

Listen to some examples of three-syllable words with pattern 3, and repeat them after the speaker.

EXAMPLES

/	–	/		/	–	/
al-	pha-	**bet**		**pho-**	to-	**graph**
bas-	ket-	**ball**		**qual-**	i-	**fy**
cat-	a-	**logue**		**re-**	cog-	**nize**
en-	ve-	**lope**		**ta-**	ble-	**cloth**
ex-	er-	**cise**		**tel-**	e-	**phone**
grad-	u-	**ate** (verb form)		**thun-**	der-	**storm**
hol-	i-	**day**				

Following are examples of four-syllable words with pattern 3. Repeat them after the speaker.

EXAMPLES

/	–	/	–		/	–	/	–
dic-	tion-	**a-**	ry		**or-**	din-	**a-**	ry
com-	pli-	**ca-**	ted		**tel-**	e-	**vi-**	sion
el-	e-	**va-**	tor					

Introducing Stress Pattern 4

Primary stress is on the second syllable and secondary stress is on the fourth syllable. All other syllables are unstressed.

Listen to the next examples of words with pattern 4, and repeat them after the speaker.

EXAMPLES

–	**/**	–	**/**	–	**/**	–	**/**
a-	**pol-**	o-	**gize**	con-	**grat-**	u-	**late**
ap-	**pre-**	ci-	ate	par-	**ti-**	ci-	**pate**

Introducing Stress Pattern 5

Secondary stress is on the first syllable and primary stress is on the second syllable. The other syllables are unstressed.

Listen to the following examples of words with pattern 5 and repeat them after the speaker.

EXAMPLES

/	**/**	–	/	**/**	–
ath-	**let-**	ic	trans-	**par-**	ent
beau-	**ti-**	cian	um-	**brel-**	la
out-	**stand-**	ing	va-	**ca-**	tion

Introducing Stress Pattern 6

Secondary stress is on the first syllable and primary stress is on the third syllable. All other syllables are unstressed.

Listen to the following examples of three-syllable words with pattern 6 and repeat them after the speaker.

EXAMPLES

/	–	**/**	/	–	**/**
af-	ter-	**noon**	gas-	o-	**line**
dis-	ap-	**pear**	Jap-	a-	**nese**
auc-	tion-	**eer**	pi-	o-	**neer**
en-	gi-	**neer**	un-	der-	**stand**

Now listen to these four-syllable words that have the same pattern. Repeat them after the speaker.

EXAMPLES

/	–	/	–
ad-	ver-	**tise-**	ment
ap-	pli-	**ca-**	tion
ar-	ti-	**fi-**	cial
ce-	le-	**bra-**	tion
dec-	o-	**ra-**	tion
e-	co-	**nom-**	ics
ed-	u-	**ca-**	tion
in-	de-	**pen-**	dence
man-	u-	**fac-**	ture
u-	ni-	**ver-**	sal

Prefixes are one- or two-syllable additions that occur at the beginning of some words. They carry certain meanings that modify the words.

The following examples contain one-syllable prefixes that are usually unstressed. Listen to the words and repeat them after the speaker.

EXAMPLES

Prefix					General meaning of prefix
		–			
co-	co-	**op-**	*er-*	**ate**	with
con-	con-	**tin-**	ue		with
com-	com-	**mit-**	tee		with
de-	de-	**liv-**	er		down, from
dis-	dis-	**cuss**			negative
ex-	ex-	**hib-**	*it*		out, from
e-	e-	**nough**			out, from
mis-	mis-	**take**			wrong
pre-	pre-	**pare**			before
pro-	pro-	**test**			for
re-	re-	**ward**			back

Other one-syllable prefixes usually have secondary stress. Listen and repeat after the speaker.

EXAMPLES

Prefix					General meaning of prefix
	ˊ				
bi-	**bi-**	**o-**	lo-	gy	two
in-	**in-**	**ept**			not
ir-	**ir-**	res-	**pon-**	si- ble	not
mal-	**mal-**	**nour-**	ish		badly
non-	**non-**	**poi-**	son-	ous	not
pan-	**pan-**	o-	**ra-**	ma	all
post-	**post-**	**pone**			after
re-	**re-**	**write**			again
sub-	**sub-**	**let**			under
trans-	**trans-**	**fer**			across
un-	**un-**	**hap-**	py		not
vice-	**vice-**	**pres-**	i-	dent	deputy

As mentioned in the preceding unit, there are prefixes that have two syllables. Here are some examples:

EXAMPLES

Prefix	General meaning
ante-	before
anti-	against
auto-	self
circum-	around
counter-	opposite to
hyper-	more than normal
hypo-	less than normal
inter-	between
micro-	tiny
mono-	one
multi-	many
poly-	many
uni-	one
ultra-	extreme

When these prefixes form a three-syllable word, there is usually primary stress on the first syllable, followed by an unstressed syllable and secondary stress on the third syllable.

Repeat the following examples after the speaker.

EXAMPLES

/	–	/	/	–	/
an-	te-	**date**	**mi-**	cro-	**scope**
an-	ti-	**freeze**	**mon-**	o-	**rail**
au-	to-	**mat**	**mul-**	ti-	**ply**
cir-	cum-	**cize**	**u-**	ni-	**verse**
coun-	ter-	**point**	**ul-**	tra-	**sound**

157

When two-syllable prefixes form a word of four or more syllables, there is usually secondary stress on the first syllable, no stress on the second, and primary stress on the third. The remaining syllables are unstressed.

Listen carefully and repeat the next examples after the speaker.

EXAMPLES

/	–	/	–	–
an-	te-	**ce-**	dent	
an-	ti-	**so-**	cial	
au-	to-	**ma-**	tic	
cir-	cum-	**ven-**	tion	
coun-	ter-	**clock-**	wise	
hy-	per-	**ac-**	tive	
hy-	po-	**der-**	mic	
in-	ter-	**ac-**	tion	
mi-	cro-	**sco-**	pic	
mon-	o-	**lin-**	gual	
po-	ly-	**es-**	ter	
u-	ni	**ver-**	sal	
mul-	ti-	**na-**	tion-	al
ul-	tra-	**vi-**	o-	let

Some exceptions to this pattern are as follows. Listen, then repeat after the speaker.

EXAMPLES

/	–	–	/
au-	to-	mo-	**bile**

/	/	–	–
an-	**ti-**	ci-	pate
an-	**ti-**	pa-	thy
an-	**tiq-**	ui-	ty
an-	**tith-**	e-	sis

/	/	–	–
mo-	**nop-**	o-	ly
mo-	**nog-**	a-	mous
mo-	**not-**	o-	ny

Suffixes are additions of one or more syllables that may be attached to the end of words. They usually have a grammatical function. For example, they can change the part of speech of a basic word, change the tense of a verb, and change the form of an adjective.

It is important to pronounce suffixes clearly, with the proper stress. They are almost always unstressed: Say the vowel sound quickly and with your mouth almost closed, but pronounce the consonant sounds in these syllables distinctly.

After the speaker, repeat the following words that end in unstressed one-syllable suffixes.

EXAMPLES

Noun suffixes		
-ance	im-**por-**	t*a*nce
-ant	im-**por-**	t*a*nt
-ate	**grad**-u-	*a*te
-ee	*e*m-**ploy-**	ee
-ence	*o*c-**cur-**	r*e*nce
-ent	**cur-**	r*e*nt
-er	**driv-**	*e*r
-ist	**so**-*cial*-	*i*st
-ment	**gov**-*e*rn-	ment
-sion	*e*x-**pan-**	s*i*on
-some	**hand-**	s*o*me
-tion	*a*t-**ten-**	t*i*on

EXAMPLES

Adjective suffixes		
		–
-al	**mu**-si-	cal
-ate	**grad**-u-	ate
-ent	**cur**-	rent
-er	**brav**-	er
-est	**brav**-	est
-ful	**help**-	ful
-ic	au-*to*-**mat**-	ic
-ive	ex-**ces**-	sive
-le	**mul**-ti-	ple
-ous	**jeal**-	ous

EXAMPLES

Verb suffixes		
		–
-ed	**want**-	ed
-es	**us**-	es
-ing	**read**-	ing

EXAMPLE

Adverb suffixes		
		–
-ly	**slow**-	ly

The following one-syllable suffixes are exceptions to the unstressed pattern. They have secondary stress. Repeat them after the speaker.

EXAMPLES

Noun suffixes			
	/	–	/
-day	**hol-**	*i-*	day
-graph	**phot-**	*o-*	graph
-tude	**at-**	*ti-*	tude

EXAMPLES

Verb suffixes			
	/	–	/
-ate	**grad-**	u-	ate
-fy	**qual-**	*i-*	fy
-ize	**crit-**	*i-*	cize

The noun suffix **-eer** has primary stress.

Repeat the next example after the speaker.

EXAMPLE

/	–	/
pi-	*o-*	**neer**

The adjective suffix **-ese** has primary stress.

Repeat the example after the speaker.

EXAMPLE

/	–	/
Jap-	a-	**nese**

Some suffixes have two syllables. Both are unstressed.

Repeat the following examples after the speaker.

EXAMPLES

Noun suffixes		–	–
-ator	**sen-**	*a-*	tor
-apher	ste-**nog-**	*ra-*	pher
-eter	ther-**mom-**	*e-*	ter
-ison	**u-**	ni-	son
-ity	na-*tion*-**al-**	*i-*	ty
-ogy	bi-**o-**	lo-	gy

EXAMPLES

Adjective suffixes		–	–
-able	**ca-**	p*a-*	ble
-ian	C*a*-**na-**	di-	*a*n
-ible	**sen-**	*si-*	ble
-ical	**rad-**	*i-*	c*al*
-ier	**pret-**	ti-	*er*
-iest	**sil-**	li-	*est*
-ior	su-**pe-**	ri-	*or*
-ory	**sen-**	*so-*	ry

EXAMPLES

Adverb suffixes		–	–
-ally	**prac-**ti-	c*al-*	ly
-ately	**pri-**	v*ate-*	ly
-ently	**per-**m*a-*	nent-	ly
-ively	com-**pe-**ti-	tive-	ly
-ously	**ser-**i-	*ous-*	ly

The following two examples are exceptions to the pattern. They have primary stress on the first syllable of the suffix. Listen and repeat the words after the speaker.

EXAMPLES

	′
(noun suffix)	**for**-**ma**-*ti*on
	′
(adverb suffix)	e-v*i*-**dent**-ly

Now repeat the following nouns that have secondary stress on the first syllable of the suffix.

EXAMPLES

′	–	′	–
in-	ven-	**to**-	ry
dic-		**ta**-	*to*r
me-	di-	**a**-	*to*r
so-	cia-	**lis**-	m

Some suffixes may cause the stress of the basic
word form to shift to another syllable. Repeat the
examples after the speaker.

EXAMPLES

– ′ – –	– – – ′ –
a-**pol**-*o*-gy	*a*-pol-*o*-**get**-ic
′ – –	– – ′ – –
cu-ri-*ous*	cu-ri-**os**-*i*-ty
– ′ – –	– – ′ –
e-**con**-*o*-my	ec-*o*-**nom**-ics
′ – –	– ′ –
i-ro-ny	i-**ron**-ic
– ′ – –	– – – ′ –
ne-**go**-ti-ate	ne-go-ti-**a**-*ti*on

```
   /  –  /            –  /  – –          –  /  – –
pho-to-graph       pho-tog-ra-pher    pho-tog-ra-phy

   /  – –             /  – /  –
pol-i-tics         pol-i-ti-cian

   /  –               –  –  /  –          /    /  – –
pub-lic            pub-li-ca-tion     pub-lic-i-ty

   /  –               –   /  –
schol-ar           scho-las-tic
```

Introducing the Patterns

When several words are spoken together in a phrase or sentence, certain words are stressed and others are spoken more softly and quickly.

Stressed Words

Four groups of words are stressed in a sentence or phrase. Say them a little louder than the unstressed words. Following are examples of sentences containing only stressed words.

1. Most <u>content</u> words—nouns, verbs, adjectives, and adverbs.

Listen to the following examples of sentences formed with only content words. Repeat each sentence, imitating the speaker's stress pattern.

EXAMPLES

> Charles Jones taught English.
> Shirley reads aloud every day.
> Aunt Janet always makes long-distance calls.
> Jason plays basketball.

2. Interrogative words—<u>who</u>, <u>whose</u>, <u>when</u>, <u>where</u>, <u>why</u>, <u>what</u>, and <u>how</u>—when they begin questions.

Repeat these examples after the speaker.

EXAMPLES

> Where's Mary's school?
> Why's Charlie leaving?
> When's Sally's party?
> Who's coming?

3. Demonstrative pronouns—<u>this</u>, <u>that</u>, <u>these</u>, and <u>those</u>—when not followed by a noun.

Listen to the next examples and repeat the examples after the speaker.

EXAMPLES

What's this?	Why're these here?
That's Jessica's ball.	We wanted those.

4. Possessive pronouns—<u>mine</u>, <u>yours</u>, <u>his</u>, <u>hers</u>, <u>ours</u>, <u>theirs</u>.

Listen to the following examples and repeat them after the speaker.

EXAMPLES

That ticket's mine.	David sold his.
This's yours.	We bought ours yesterday.
Barbara got hers.	They gave theirs away.

Unstressed Words

There is no stress on most function words in a phrase or sentence. Here, you will find them broken down into 13 groups. Say them quickly with an unstressed vowel, but be sure to pronounce the consonants clearly. The unstressed words are printed in *italics*.

Do not stress:

1. The articles <u>a</u>, <u>an</u>, <u>the</u>.

Listen to your tape and repeat these examples after the speaker, trying to imitate the speaker's stress pattern.

EXAMPLES

a dog	*an* apple	*the* chair

2. Prepositions, such as <u>to</u>, <u>from</u>, <u>with</u>, <u>in</u>, <u>on</u>, <u>through</u>, <u>for</u>, <u>by</u>, <u>over</u>, <u>under</u>, etc.

Repeat the following examples after the speaker.

EXAMPLES

for a dog	*to the* hospital
with an apple	*around the* room
on the chair	*over the* hill
in the house	*after the* concert
through the door	*before the* show
of a family	

3. The subject pronouns <u>I</u>, <u>you</u>, <u>he</u>, <u>she</u>, <u>it</u>, <u>we</u>, and <u>they</u>.

Repeat these examples after the speaker.

EXAMPLES

I know *the* lesson.
You found *the* book *on the* shelf.
She tells secrets *to* everybody.
He talks *on the* phone too much.
We eat fish *on* Fridays.
They travel *to* Europe *a* lot.

4. The possessive pronouns <u>my</u>, <u>your</u>, <u>his</u>, <u>her</u>, <u>our</u>, <u>their</u>.

Repeat these examples after the speaker.

EXAMPLES

my car	*her* dress	*our* house
your friend	*his* brother	*their* camera

5. The object pronouns <u>me</u>, <u>you</u>, <u>her</u>, <u>him</u>, <u>us</u>, <u>them</u>.

Repeat the following examples after the speaker.

EXAMPLES

I saw *him*.	They warned *you*.
They told *me*.	My dad helped *us*.
We asked *her*.	Put *them on the* table.

6. The demonstrative adjectives—<u>this</u>, <u>that</u>, <u>these</u>, and <u>those</u>—when followed by a noun.

Repeat the next examples after the speaker.

EXAMPLES

This book *is* interesting.
She bought *that* house.
We like *these* shoes.
Those boys talk too loud.

7. Forms of the verb <u>be</u>—<u>am</u>, <u>are</u>, <u>is</u>, <u>was</u>, <u>were</u>, <u>aren't</u>, <u>isn't</u>, <u>wasn't</u>, <u>weren't</u>.

Say the following examples after the speaker.

EXAMPLES

I *am* here.	We *were in the* garden.
He *is a* tall man.	He *wasn't* late.
They *are* all sick.	

8. The expressions <u>there is</u> and <u>there are</u>.

Repeat the examples after the speaker.

EXAMPLES

There is a car *in the* driveway.
There is one apple *in the* basket.
There is jewelry *in that* box.
There are too many cars *on the* road.
There are five people *in the* family.

9. The <u>to</u> before a verb.

Say the following examples after the speaker.

EXAMPLES

> *He* needs *to* work.
> *I* like *to* eat early.
> *My* mother loves *to* cook.
> *We* want *to* see *the* whole movie.

10. Auxiliary verbs, such as <u>am</u>, <u>is</u>, <u>are</u>, <u>was</u>, <u>were</u>, <u>do</u>, <u>does</u>, <u>did</u>, <u>have</u>, <u>has</u>, <u>had</u>, <u>isn't</u>, <u>wasn't</u>, <u>didn't</u>, etc.

Listen to the following examples and repeat them after the speaker.

EXAMPLES

> I *am* working *in the* house.
> She *is* talking *on the* phone.
> He *was* helping *them*.
> When *do* we start school?
> Why *does* he travel so much?
> *Have* you done *your* work?
> We *have been* working all day.
> He *had* always told *the* truth.
> They *had* had *a* bad day.

11. Modal auxiliaries, such as <u>can</u>, <u>must</u>, <u>have to</u>, <u>should</u>, <u>could</u>, <u>would</u>, etc.

Repeat these examples after the speaker.

EXAMPLES

> John *can* come.
> Joe *has to* work.
> Sam *should* leave.
> We *would like to* help.
> You *mustn't* go *in the* street.
> Kathy *doesn't have to* work.

12. <u>Who</u>, <u>whose</u>, <u>when</u>, <u>where</u>, <u>why</u>, <u>what</u>, and <u>how</u> in the middle of a sentence.

Listen to these examples and repeat them after the speaker.

EXAMPLES

> Jenny has *a* cousin *whose* name *is* Smith.
> *Do you* know *where she* lives?
> Only Courtney knows *why she* said that.
> *He didn't* tell *me when to* come.
> *I can* figure out *how to* do *it.*

13. Other short function words, such as <u>and</u>, <u>but</u>, <u>or</u>, <u>so</u>, <u>not</u>, <u>if</u>, <u>as</u>, <u>because</u>, <u>whether</u>, <u>since</u>, <u>until</u>, <u>though</u>, <u>although</u>.

Repeat the following examples after the speaker.

EXAMPLES

> Mary *and* Bob have plenty *of* food, *such as* sand-
> wiches, cakes, *and* cookies.
> Joe, *not* John, *has been* here *since* noon.
> Scott *was* worried *because his* wife *was so* late.
> *I'll* stay *until he* calls, *then I'll* leave *so you*
> *can* study.
> *Although you're* sick, *you can* eat *with* Carolyn
> *or* Sue.
> *I don't* know *whether he was* late *or* not.
> *If you* eat that much, *you'll be as* sick *as a* dog.

Exceptions

- The negative modal, <u>can't</u>, is usually stressed.
- When auxiliary verbs and modal auxiliaries are not followed by a verb, they have strong stress.

Listen to the following examples and repeat them after the speaker.

EXAMPLES

> *She* can't help *him with the* cooking.
> *I'll* come *to the* party *if I* can.
> *We would* lend *you the* car *if we* could.
> Carol has *a* new car, *but* Margaret doesn't.
> *He doesn't* know *I'm* unhappy, *but I* am.

Practice for Mastery

Now practice the stress patterns discussed in this unit by repeating the following sentences after the speaker.

EXAMPLES

> *The* money *is in the* bank.
> *He* came over *to* talk *to me.*
> *She can* help *him with the* cooking.
> *I should* buy *a* new dress *for the* wedding.
> *We could* lend *you our* car.
> *I will* send *you a* letter tomorrow.
> *They're* walking *to the* store.
> *He didn't* work *because he was* sick.
> Karen *and* Danny stayed *until they* knew
> *whether or not* Val *was* coming.

- Any word can be given extra stress to emphasize or clarify a statement.

In the examples that follow, emphasis is shown in boldface. Listen, and repeat each sentence after the speaker.

EXAMPLES

	Meaning
I wanted to go to the **circus**.	(not the **movies**.)
They didn't go to **France**.	(They went to Paris, **Virginia**!)
I lost my ring on my way **to** the store.	(not **from** the store.)
He gave her the money.	(**I** didn't give her the money.)
He **gave** her the money.	(He didn't **lend** her the money.)
He gave **her** the money.	(He didn't give the money to **me**.)
He gave her the **money**.	(He didn't give her the **car**.)

Be careful not to use extra stress if you do not intend special meaning.

Next, listen to the following paragraph, paying close attention to the stress patterns.

Learning to speak a language is a little like learning to dance. They both take a long time to master, but are fun from the beginning. Both require interaction with another person, who is saying or doing something different. Fluent speakers and good dancers don't have to think about their skills. They perform them naturally. To acquire these skills, you need a lot of practice and patience. Encouragement from someone else helps a great deal.

Now, repeat the paragraph, one phrase at a time, after the speaker.

Learning *to* speak
a language
is a little *like*
learning *to* dance.
They both take *a* long time
to master,
but are fun
from the beginning.
Both require interaction
with another person,
who is saying *or* doing
something different.
Fluent speakers
and good dancers
don't have to think
about their skills.
They perform *them* naturally.
To acquire *these* skills,
you need *a* lot *of* practice
and patience.
Encouragement *from* someone else
helps *a* great deal.

Read the paragraph aloud again, practicing the proper stress. Try recording your reading on tape to see if it sounds natural.

Here is another paragraph. Listen to it on your tape, noting the speaker's stress patterns.

Last May we had a surprise party at my house for one of my friends. It was his fifti-eth birthday. We invited about thirty people, and most of them were able to come. One couple even traveled all the way from New Jersey. Several people who had been away for a long time were here. Most of the guests hadn't met each other before the party, but they were having a wonderful time talking during the half-hour before the birthday man arrived. It seemed that a very special

person was a magnet for other special people. When he got here, he was really surprised, and happy to see so many friends. It
was a good party.

Now, repeat each phrase after the speaker.

Last May
we had *a* surprise party
at my house
for one *of my* friends.
It was his fiftieth birthday.
We invited *about* thirty people,
and most *of them*
were able *to* come.
One couple *even* traveled
all *the* way *from* New Jersey.
Several people
who had been away
for a long time
were here.
Most *of the* guests
hadn't met each other
before the party,
but they were having
a wonderful time talking
during the half-hour
before the birthday man arrived.
It seemed
that a very special person
was a magnet
for other special people.
When he got here,
he was really surprised,
and happy *to* see
so many friends.
It was a good party.

Read the paragraph aloud again, comparing your
stresses with those of the speaker.

PART FOUR
INTONATION
PATTERNS

Intonation is the "musical score" of a language. Each "tune" has a special meaning. In the following units, the intonation patterns are represented graphically: A horizontal line means that the words are all delivered at approximately the same pitch level; a rising line means that the pitch rises; a descending line means that it falls.

Pattern ___◣.

On your tape, listen to the intonation pattern in the following examples, and repeat them after the speaker.

EXAMPLES

Good morning.	Be careful.
Good afternoon.	Drive safely.
Good evening.	Say hello to your mother.
Good night.	Goodbye.
Hello.	Bye.
Hi.	Thank you.
Excuse me.	You're welcome.
Take care.	See you later.

When you say the name of the person you are talking to, add a second pattern to the previous greeting: ___◢.

Now, repeat these phrases.

EXAMPLES

Good morning, Bill.
Good evening, Miss Jones.
Be careful, Emily.
Say hello to your mother, John.

Introducing the Patterns

Pattern 1: ___/\.

Listen to the speaker's intonation pattern in the following examples of one-phrase sentences, then repeat each sentence after the speaker.

EXAMPLES

She's my sister.	I have a dog.
They're from Venezuela.	It's beautiful.
We're going to visit them.	We love it.
He's here.	

Pattern 2: ___/ ___/\.

Listen to the following examples of two-phrase sentences, and repeat them after the speaker.

EXAMPLES

He's here, but she isn't.
I have a dog, and you have a cat.
She's my sister, and he's my cousin.
When I see him, I'll tell him.
After you get here, have a cup of coffee.
Before you start, take a deep breath.

Introducing the Patterns

Pattern 1: Tag Questions ___/\ __/?

This is the same pattern used for a greeting followed by a name. (See Unit Thirty-eight.)

Listen to and repeat each of the following sentences after the speaker.

EXAMPLES

> He's coming, isn't he?
> You're a lawyer, aren't you?
> My sister told you, didn't she?
> You'll come to my party, won't you?

Pattern 2: Tag Questions Indicating Displeasure ___/\ ‾‾\ ?

A message of displeasure can be conveyed through a different intonation pattern. Listen to the same sentences, noting the change in the speaker's tone and repeat each question after the speaker.

EXAMPLES

> He's coming, isn't he?
> You're a lawyer, aren't you?
> My sister told you, didn't she?
> You'll come to my party, won't you?

This pattern can also indicate confidence in the response.

As before, repeat the example.

EXAMPLE

> The water's nice, isn't it?

Pattern 3: Questions with Question Words⎯⋀?

You will note that this is the same pattern as that used in greetings and one-phrase statements. Try to imitate the speaker's tone.

Listen to and repeat each sentence after the speaker.

EXAMPLES

> When are you going?   Why are you crying?
> Who is the teacher?   Where did he go?

When an answer to your question is suggested, it is on a higher tone: ⎯⎯⋀ ⎯⎯⁄

As before, repeat these examples after the speaker.

EXAMPLES

> When are you going, Friday?
> Who is the teacher, Miss Smith?
> Why are you crying, to make me feel bad?
> Where did he go, to the movies?

The answers to the preceding questions have their own pattern: ⎯⟍ . (pause) ⎯⟍ .

Repeat these examples after the speaker.

EXAMPLES

> Yes. Friday.   No. I can't help it.
> No. Miss Jones.   Yes. To the movies.

Pattern 4: Questions Indicating Annoyance ⌐\ ?

Next, repeat these questions that show annoyance through the intonation pattern.

EXAMPLES

> Why do you ask?
> When is he coming?
> Where did you hear that?
> Who did this to you?

Pattern 5: Questions Without Question Words ___/ ?

Here is the last set of questions. As before, repeat each one after the speaker.

EXAMPLES

Are you happy?	Was she there?
Will he win?	Were they hurt?
Do you like it?	Did you see it?

Introducing the Patterns

Fundamentally, the intonation pattern used in counting and listing is a series of level and rising tones that end with a final drop in pitch.

Counting

Listen to your tape and repeat the following examples after the speaker.

EXAMPLES

> One, two, three, four, five.
>
> Four hundred and thirty-seven, four hundred and thirty-eight, four hundred and thirty-nine, four hundred and forty.

Listing

As before, repeat these examples after the speaker.

EXAMPLES

> I need shoes, socks, shirts, and pants.
>
> He ate two hamburgers, french fries, and an ice cream cone.
>
> She likes perfume, chocolates, flowers, and money.

Introducing the Patterns

Pattern 1: When the Question Requires a "Yes" or "No" Answer

Listen to your tape and repeat the questions after the speaker. Then listen for and repeat the answers.

EXAMPLES

Question	Answer
Would you like potatoes or carrots?	No, I would rather have fruit.
Are you unhappy or uncomfortable?	No, I feel just fine.
Will he eat ice cream or cake?	Yes, he probably will (but he should be on a diet).
Would you like a drink or something?	Yes, please, I'm thirsty.

Pattern 2: When the Question Offers a Limited Choice

EXAMPLES

Questions	Answers
Would you like potatoes or carrots?	I would like carrots.
Are you unhappy or uncomfortable?	I'm unhappy.
Will he eat ice cream or cake?	He'll have cake.

Practice in Context

Listen to the following dialogues on your tape and repeat each line after the speaker.

1. — Can you help me with these boxes, Steve?
   — No. I can't.
   — Why not?
   — They're too heavy. I hurt my back and I'm not supposed to lift anything heavy.
   — Well . . . how am I going to get them upstairs?
   — Call John and see if he'll help you!

2. — Hi, Carol. How are you?
   — Fine, thanks. How are you Ms. Johnson?
   — Fine. How's school these days?
   — Oh . . . it's O.K. but we have too much homework!
   — Are you going to the game?
   — Yes, are you?
   — No. I have to clean the garage.
   — O.K. . . . see you later.
   — Bye, drive carefully!

3. — Where are you going, Mom?
   — To the movies. Do you want to come?
   — Oh . . . I'd love to, but I have to go to the library.
   — The library! Wow! I'm really proud of you. Are you doing research?
   — No . . . I'm going to pick up my friends. They need a ride home.

4. — Come live with me in the city. You'll have lots of fun.
   — I don't like the city. It's too noisy. There's too much traffic and pollution, and there's no place to park. Why don't you come live with me in the country?
   — I hate the country. It's too far away, and there's more traffic out there than in the city. Besides, there's nothing to do there. Don't you get bored?
   — You're looking for an argument, aren't you? I can see we weren't meant for each other.
   — Don't be silly! I think this is a perfect relationship. I really like living alone.